Haunted
Lighthouses

George C. Steitz

Pineapple Press, Inc.
Sarasota, Florida

To Susan

Inquiries should be addressed to:

Pineapple Press, Inc.
P.O. Box 3889
Sarasota, Florida 34230
www.pineapplepress.com

Library of Congress Cataloging-in-Publication Data

Steitz, George C.
    Haunted lighthouses and how to find them / George C. Steitz.—1st ed.
cm.
        ISBN 1-56164-268-1 (pbk. : alk. paper)
        1. Ghosts—United States. 2. Haunted places—United States. 3. Lighthouses—United States—Miscellanea. I. Title.

BF1472.U6 S74 2002
133.1'22—dc21
                                                                    2002029319

First Edition
10 9 8 7 6 5 4 3 2 1

Design by Shé Sicks
Printed in the United States of America

Contents

Acknowledgments v

Foreword vii

Introduction 1

Florida

   Wandering Souls 5

      —∾— St. Augustine Lighthouse

         Travel Tips 35

   The Eternal Bloodstain 46

      —∾— Pensacola Lighthouse

         Travel Tips 65

Georgia

   Phantom Footfalls 68

      —∾— St. Simons Island Lighthouse

         Travel Tips 86

Maryland

   America's Most Haunted Lighthouse 92

      —∾— Point Lookout Lighthouse

         Travel Tips 114

Connecticut

   Ernie the Ghost 119

      —∾— New London Ledge Light

         Travel Tips 134

Massachusetts

Haunted Harbor   140

—∾— Boston Lighthouse

Travel Tips   160

Haunted Eyes   163

—∾— Plymouth Lighthouse

Travel Tips   181

Maine

A Deadly Melody   187

—∾— Seguin Island Lighthouse

Travel Tips   202

Michigan

Ghost of a Sea Captain   209

—∾— White River Light Station

Travel Tips   224

Ghost Light   229

—∾— Old Presque Isle Lighthouse

Travel Tips   239

Acknowledgments

It is with much gratitude that I acknowledge the many people who have given generously of their time and knowledge.

In no particular order, but all of special importance, thanks to Elinor De Wire, author of *Guardians of the Lights*. Elinor may not believe in ghosts, but she tells a great ghost story, and she sure knows her lighthouses.

I thank Bill Thomson, author of *New England's Haunted Lighthouses,* a friend who suggested I write this book, and Lee Holloway for her help with research. Thanks to Mark Nesbitt, author of *Ghosts of Gettysburg,* Don Hammett at Point Lookout, and Laura Berg, who spent two years living with ghosts and survived to tell about it.

At the lighthouses, I was helped immensely by: Kathy Fleming (St. Augustine Lighthouse and Museum); Linda King (St. Simons Island Lighthouse); Karen O'Donnell (White River Light Station); Richard Himelrich (Boston Harbor Light); Philip Jermain (Seguin Island Light). I thank Lorraine Parris for telling her moving story, and Bob Shanklin for sharing his compelling one.

Thanks to Brae Rafferty at New London Ledge Light, Dan Holiday, David Lapham, and Karen Harvey in St. Augustine, and New England's Grand Lady, Connie Small. Thanks also to John Forbes at Friends of Boston Harbor, Michael Humphries, and

Donnie Hammett at Point Lookout. I am indebted to many others at each location for their valuable help.

Finally, on the network TV side, I am grateful to Sandra Gregory, a terrific executive producer, the traveling crew including Rich Schutte, and David Belko, a good friend in the edit suite.

Foreword

Lighthouses are among the oldest structures in America. Like the castles of Europe, they are proud, sturdy, mystical—and sometimes even haunted. But as storms gobble up the shoreline and water edges closer, lighthouses are in danger, and time is running out for many of them.

Preserving the legends and lore that surround lighthouses is one way we can help save them from extinction. *Haunted Lighthouses and How to Find Them* goes a long way toward raising our awareness and enhancing our appreciation for these historic treasures. There's a lot of love for lighthouses expressed in its pages as the author brings ghost stories and legends to life. Many have been handed down by mariners, Coast Guardsmen, and even lighthouse keepers themselves.

Ghostly lighthouse tales are genuinely a form of oral history. I can't think of one of these lighthouse legends that doesn't make a worthwhile contribution—an important historical fact, for example, or a significant detail about the people and places of the past. The basis for many of the stories you're about to read is the lighthouse keeper's dedication amidst the hardships many keepers and their families were forced to endure. Often with great sacrifice, women helped keep the lights burning, and you'll come away with a better understanding of their service and commitment.

Haunted Lighthouses and How to Find Them is a book for the ghost buff, the lover of lighthouses, or the traveler looking for a unique place to visit. Along with chilling accounts of hauntings and fascinating glimpses of early lighthouse life, it's filled with helpful information about locating the lighthouses, and where to stay and what to see once you find them. It's fun to read and will surely pique your curiosity to learn and discover more.

We need to keep lighthouses in the front of our minds, to keep reading about them and paying visits whenever we can, and supporting organizations like the American Lighthouse Foundation in their efforts to save not only the structures, but the history and folklore associated with them. Finally, we need to keep spinning the yarns and passing down the legends, helping to insure that lighthouses will go on shining for many generations to come.

—Tim Harrison

President, American Lighthouse Foundation

Contact:

American Lighthouse Foundation

P.O. Box 889

Wells, Maine 04090

www.lighthousefoundation.org

Introduction

I met the Scotsman on the morning of the murder. He was chatting with fellow tourists, a busload of hearty seniors who had braved the lousy weather. They had all arrived early to poke around the lighthouse, which at a little past eight o'clock in the morning was still bathed in wet, soupy fog.

Swirls of yellowish mist rose up off the rocks like smoke curling around a dying fire. Swords of light from the beacon slashed through the thick morning air. From somewhere unseen the doleful sound of an electric motor hummed, straining to power the revolving lens. Every few seconds a piercing foghorn blast punctured the air. It was enough to make anyone edgy—even the gulls seemed restless. But edgy and restless are good when you're planning a homicide.

The morning was gray, misty, and damp. The Scotsman stamped his feet to chase the chill from his toes. Others breathed into their cupped hands and shivered. They were miserable and trying to look nonchalant about it. What they were more than anything was curious. And who can blame them for wanting to know what all our fussing was about. Tentatively, they drifted toward us; furtively, they glanced our way, inching closer. Was it suspicion I detected in their eyes, or confusion?

What we were doing—and what they were trying to figure out—was shooting a scene for the network television special

Haunted Lighthouses. And a grisly scene it was—one depicting a legendary nineteenth-century ax murder. We had selected this isolated island off the coast of Maine as the perfect setting for our concocted tragedy, and we were trying our best to pull it off. But the fog was killing us, so to speak. We had yearned for fog, but not this much; bleak we wanted, but not this bleak. And where was our actress—the one portraying the lighthouse keeper's wife and victim of his murderous rage? My cell phone vibrated. The young lady was stranded at her hotel on the mainland. Of all things, she was fogged in. Otherwise we were set to go. Cameras, crew, ax, fake blood, ruthless lighthouse keeper—and plenty of fog—all standing by.

Impatiently, I gave the order—roll film. Shoot around the missing woman. We'll fix it in the edit—the credo of producers on tight budgets.

But what about the Scotsman, where does he fit? He gave me an idea. This thoughtful, distinguished, crimson-faced gentleman was the only tourist who actually spoke to us. He asked us what we were filming. And the answer caused him to let go of a big, throaty chuckle.

"Ahhh, haunted lighthouses, is it? That's a good one. Over where I come from we have our castles. And every castle has a ghost. But here in America, I guess you have your haunted lighthouses." Another big chuckle was hurled my way.

It wasn't the last time I'd hear the comparison, that lighthouses are to America what castles are to Europe, but it was the first. And right there on-the-spot I embraced this allusion as the theme for the opening segment of our film.

The Scotsman wandered off, the actress finally showed up, and much later, we were able to fix everything in the edit. The morning hadn't been so bad, after all.

After many months and a dozen or so lighthouses under our belts, I came to consider the Scotsman's off-handed remark prophetic.

Lighthouses *are* like castles—romantic reminders of American history. They symbolize a part of our past that we yearn to keep while it sadly slips from our grasp. And haunted or not, just gazing up at a lofty lighthouse can raise the gooseflesh and warm the soul.

What better place to discover a good old-fashioned American ghost rattling around?

Wandering Souls
St. Augustine Lighthouse

Florida

America's oldest city is one of its most haunted. A ghostly presence hangs over St. Augustine, Florida, as thick as Spanish moss. Every night on its mystical shores, spirits arise from musty tombs and dark corners. They creep and float and ooze out of secret hiding places—places that you and I would never guess were even there.

As your imagination begins to wander freely and you prepare to follow, find your way to the most haunted place of all—St. Augustine Lighthouse.

Photo by David Nowicki

At night, the powerful beam of St. Augustine Lighthouse is visible for nineteen miles. Ghosts are sometimes visible within the lighthouse itself.

"This lighthouse is really cool!" A young visitor shouts up at the mid-afternoon sky with delight. "It's *s-o-o-o* tall it makes you dizzy just looking at it," she declares, leaning backwards and stumbling playfully to make her point.

Everyone's impressed. St. Augustine Lighthouse is a knockout—a perfect ten. In addition to serving the north Florida coast with its powerful light beacon, the tower itself is a brilliant daymark. Its striking black and white spiral bands, nearly identical to its more famous sister lighthouse at Cape Hatteras, North Carolina, make it a dazzling marker for boats and aircraft.

What delighted that young girl was the size of the tower—but without the paint-job, it's not nearly so awesome. And it's not just the broad stripes. Topping it all off is a lantern roof done in brilliant blood red and trimmed in gleaming, yellow brass—bringing to mind a giant ancient soldier boldly painted up for war.

This is Anastasia Island, just outside St. Augustine. It's mid-afternoon on a cool, blue weekday in spring. The lighthouse, 161-feet tall, is swaying slightly in a gentle breeze. I'm standing in its long shadow, waiting on the grassy apron around its heavy base, watching for a sign that the scheduled tour of the lighthouse and keeper's cottage is about to begin. No ordinary one, either—it's the *ghost* tour.

Finally, the announcement is made by a young man who appears out of nowhere wearing baggy, old-fashioned pants with suspenders and a grin from ear to ear. He steps down off the wooden back porch of the Victorian keeper's dwelling and shouts, "Everyone on the two o'clock tour please step over here." He points to a tall trellis with a wide gate in the white picket fence that encloses the sprawling lighthouse compound.

I enter under the trellis in the company of a small party of wide-eyed tourists—*other* wide-eyed tourists, since I'm pretty intrigued myself. Like sheep we funnel through the gate as the young man herds us along. A little tittering gives us away as first timers. There's about ten people in the group and we start to mingle.

Of course, there's the initial curiosity about us—the people I travel with—one with broadcast video camera and the other with a fuzzy-coated microphone on the end of a long boom pole. The "mic" is wearing this furry coat for a reason—it's a wind screen—but it looks silly and gets everyone giggling. Our strange paraphernalia always gets a lot of attention, but soon the excitement dies down.

The three of us—camera operator, soundman, and me, the producer—are under contract with a national cable network. We're here to videotape a ghost tour then spice it up with interesting interviews, all for an upcoming TV special called *Haunted Lighthouses*. Today, if things go as expected, people will give us the once over, ask a few questions, then shrug. We'll fade into the woodwork, and that's how we get the job done.

The group assembles near the cottage entrance. On the subject of ghosts, my new friends might fall anywhere from true believer to good-natured skeptic. But everyone's here to have some fun and maybe discover what, if anything, is stirring at St. Augustine Lighthouse.

Ghosts or no ghosts, this is still one of the finest-looking light-houses in America—great to photograph or just to admire. Before going inside, I take one more look at the venerable tower. I'd like to shout and give it a salute. Of course, the whispers bring us here today.

Kathy Fleming, lighthouse and museum director, greets us at the door. Her soft, honey-toned voice is so welcoming it's like we just dropped by her home to pay our respects. Kathy is one of those rare people with the talent to give you a real sense of importance—like you're the most critical part of her day, despite that desk full of paperwork she left upstairs.

Kathy introduces herself by shaking hands all around. She begins the tour with a brief history of the lighthouse. On October 15, 1874, the first keeper proudly lighted the beacon, the most pow-erful light of its kind anywhere. Ships as far away as nineteen miles could see the glow of this technical marvel. For its brilliant illumi-nation, it depended on a first-order Fresnel lens.

Although not supernatural, the subject of the Fresnel (pro-nounced "fraynel") lens is a fascinating one, and one that also involves a phenomenon for which we have no explanation. In the late eighteenth century, a frail, slow-witted boy was totally written off at age eight. He couldn't read or remember his lessons. Despite his early failures, Augustin-Jean Fresnel developed a lens that revo-lutionized lighthouses and is still in use today. The story of his life was a mystery about misunderstood genius and cruelty.

Starting in 1874, St. Augustine Lighthouse became a glowing example of Fresnel's work. But the task of keeping a light in those days could be backbreaking work. Every night the lighthouse keeper was expected to carry a gallon bucket of kerosene in each hand and trudge up the steep steps to the lantern room, where he trimmed the wicks and prepared the lights. Then at daybreak came another climb to the top to draw curtains to protect the delicate lens prisms from the blazing sun.

This was grueling work, and perhaps it was the exercise that proved too taxing for the first keeper. Or perhaps it was something else. The actual cause of his death isn't known. His name was William Harn and he served here just long enough to develop a fondness for the beacon. One night while dragging a load of kerosene up the spiral steps, Harn keeled over and died. Did he fall down the stairs and break his neck? Struck by a heart attack, or worse, was he murdered? We know only that his demise was sudden and unexpected. Behind him he left a grieving widow, six young children, and a brand new lighthouse in need of tending. He dearly loved them all.

A simple stone in St. Augustine's moss-covered Evergreen Cemetery marks the grave where Keeper William Harn was put down to rest in peace. Kathy shows us an old black and white picture of the grave. With a devilish smile and twitch of her nose, she sighs, "But is Keeper Harn *really* resting in peace?"

"If you ask certain people that question," she declares, "the answer may surprise you." The way she puts it, it's a sure bet she considers herself one of *those* people.

Kathy nudges us toward a trap door, actually a large hole cut in the hardwood floor of what used to be the keeper's dining room. To lighten the mood, she lowers her voice and swaggers. "To the basement," she commands. Down and down we travel on twisting wooden steps, tightly gripping a handhold of thick hemp rope, glancing furtively into a deep, dark cistern at the foot of the stairs. Into the dank lighthouse basement we follow Kathy.

The ceiling is low and there's a chill in the thick, moist air. The temperature has dropped at least twenty degrees. Does that account for the little quivers in the spine? Perhaps it's the sudden change of temperature, or maybe something else—a presence? Specifically the presence of Keeper Harn's spirit.

"A ghost might feel a little more connected to the earth if it knew something had been left behind—something important." Kathy delivers this with a little shudder. Sudden deaths are often thought to result in hauntings. Violent deaths even more so. We know Keeper Harn died suddenly, and we can surmise he wasn't really ready to go. But is that enough to generate a ghostly presence after death?

And did Kathy Fleming just say *ghost*? This *is* an official ghost tour, after all, but hearing her use the word for the first time is a little jarring. You'd imagine her expounding on the brilliance of Frenchman Augustin-Jean Fresnel's lens. But *ghosts*?

Here she was, though, a well-respected lighthouse historian, hinting at the existence of something as nonacademic as a ghost. So when Kathy declares that she suspects Keeper Harn's spirit might still be wandering around the property, it gives us pause—even a reason to reconsider those nagging doubts about the substance of ghost stories.

But it turns out Kathy has had her own ghostly encounter—a *personal* experience, she calls it. The tour is just underway and already it seems as if we're getting more than we'd bargained for. This little group of tourists is all ears, camera crew included.

In nearly a whisper, Kathy takes us back in time to a chilly winter night about a year earlier. The wind was howling and Florida suddenly felt more like Maine. Of all nights, Kathy was expected to work late on this one. As the hours passed and darkness fell, she decided to close up with a routine check of the facility. It was during that inspection when Kathy glimpsed something no one has been able to explain, least of all Kathy herself.

She gathers us close and we fall in tightly around her. The hush in her voice floats on the deadly silence of the room.

Why are we all whispering, anyway? Who are we trying not to disturb?

"It was just after eight. In wintertime the basement can get pretty dark at that hour," Kathy notes. "And awfully intimidating."

We believe her. It's intimidating enough in the middle of the afternoon. The heavy walls of deep red brick are dimly lit with a couple of bare bulbs, and shadows seem to grow everywhere and nowhere at every turn. There's the mosquito-like electric hum of some unseen motor, a well or pump. It's unnerving. This place could easily get under your skin.

Kathy continues her story. She was on her way to the basement. Down the wooden steps she went, across the cold cement floor, her footsteps pounding and causing an echo behind her. She felt her way through the thick darkness in the familiar passageway. It was creepy, but no creepier than usual, she tells us.

So far, Kathy sensed nothing out of the ordinary. She entered a long, narrow hallway leading to the dark video room about twenty feet ahead. She felt utterly alone and helpless, but that was a feeling everyone seemed to get down here. The stories about the ghosts in this basement were famous, but Kathy resisted their spells.

She can't remember what happened first. The hair on her arms standing straight up among the tiny goosebumps? The shiver up her spine or the sudden heartbeat leaping in her chest? Perhaps everything happened at once.

Kathy jerked to a stop. But there was nothing there. Just a light—a light spilling out from under a closed closet door beside her. *That was strange,* she thought. *It was just a storage closet and the door was always kept locked. Why was the light on?*

Calm down, she told herself. *This is no big deal. I'll unlock the closet, turn off the light and get out of here fast.*

Kathy fumbled with her keys and inserted one into the lock. It turned with a noisy jiggle, but what was that other sound? She stood absolutely still, feet frozen to the cold cement floor. That's when she saw something move.

Out of the corner of her eye she saw a figure. It looked like a man. But who, and how? The lighthouse had been closed for hours. Slowly turning her head toward the room at the end of the hall, she found herself staring at a large, shadowy image. In fact, it was a very tall and thin man. His face was heavily lined, his eye sockets were darker than the rest of him, and he was attired in what Kathy perceived to be an old-fashioned lighthouse uniform. The man stood rigidly in the doorway. She heard him breathing.

Fear swept over her. She was alone with a strange man in the dark basement of the house. His shadow seemed to pulse with every breath, growing larger then smaller as his chest heaved. He didn't move or speak, but the shadows moved. Spiderlike, a dark area crept up the walls and across the ceiling. Kathy demonstrates to us by waving her arms to make her own shadow dance on the red brick wall.

In a quiet voice she describes for us the man's uniform. She saw the glint of his brass buttons and gold braiding on his sleeve. No mistaking it for anything but a lighthouse keeper's coat.

As best as Kathy can recollect, a few seconds later, or perhaps it was an entire minute—she doesn't know how long they stood staring at one another—he turned and retreated into the room. She watched his shadow melt into the darkness.

"I thought I must have forgotten someone down here and I'd

just go in and say, sir, we're getting ready to close, so come on out now."

Kathy called out, but there was no response. *Sir, please come out now. Sir!* She pretty nearly barked the order at him. She didn't know what else to call him but "sir." Tentatively, she edged down the hall to investigate. Approaching the doorway where the man had appeared just moments before, Kathy slowly stepped into the room.

"There was nobody there. When I walked in, no one was there," she declares. "The room was completely empty."

Something crept up her spine. It creeps up mine, too. The only way out of this room is past the spot where she was standing.

Kathy leads us into the room, and we follow like mice creeping past a sleeping cat. It's a small area, not much more than the corner of a slightly musty underground space. "It's our video room," Kathy explains. Sure enough, there's a small television monitor and a few cassette tapes strewn about.

For some time, all members of our group stand there, moving nothing but our eyes, casting looks at different corners of the room, searching for who knows what—a secret place where Kathy's mysterious man might have hidden? Where could he have gone?

That's precisely the question that has haunted Kathy Fleming since her brush with the unknown on that cold, dark night the previous winter.

A shy but curious person in the group finally speaks up, but with a stutter in a low, timid voice: "Who . . . who was it in the room?"

By the time the question is out, Kathy is halfway up the twisting stairs and out of the basement. She turns her head, smiles and responds. "I don't know. I don't have any idea." She finishes her climb out through the hatch, then disappears. Behind her she's left a bunch of puzzled, blank stares. Perhaps she just remembered that desk full of unfinished paperwork. We didn't see Kathy again that day.

But we don't remain alone for long. Karen Harvey meets us at the top of the spiral staircase. Karen is a journalist who once worked for the local newspaper. She's the author of a book about haunted places in Florida. Where Kathy Fleming left off, Karen picks up. We don't miss a beat.

With Karen we meander over to the lightkeeper's dwelling immediately behind the lighthouse. It's only about a hundred feet away through the thick grass. Karen leads us up the steep wooden stairs, across the second floor terrace that runs along the outside of the double-deck building, and stops at a tall window flanked by two huge, black shutters. She points into the room. "Right in there a man hanged himself," she declares.

The lightkeeper's house, which is believed to have been built in 1873, about the same time as the lighthouse, was gutted by fire in 1971. The blaze was devastating, nearly burning the original wooden timbers of this building to the ground.

"The building was a burned out shell from the 1970s to the early 1980s," Karen explains "That's when the restoration work began—an effort sponsored by the Junior Service League to rebuild the house to its original nineteenth-century appearance."

Documents found in the lighthouse identify the foreman of the job as Michael Gourley. In a publication called *Skylight*, dated October 1985, Gourley is quoted in accounts of several strange incidents that occurred within three successive days after starting the restoration. All three seem to involve powerfully violent acts.

"A beam fell and impaled one of the men in the arm," reported Gourley. In a second incident, he said: "A stump we were cutting flew up and struck another man right between the eyes." A third event he noted was when a tree catapulted off a chain and flew into the rear window of a truck.

Could these unexplained occurrences have been supernatural warnings? Signs that someone or something wasn't happy with what was going on? That's exactly what many people believe. Ever since the old wooden structure was exposed by fire, there have been reports of people claiming to feel uneasy in the house—and some were actually so terrified they had to leave immediately. Such was the case of a construction worker who saw a limp body dangling from a beam in the ceiling.

"In the early phase of the restoration project, one worker was on scaffolding, right here where we are standing," says Karen. "He was working on the porch roof, his back to the window, and he felt a presence behind him. He turned and saw a man hanging from one of those beams."

We peer through the glass. The beams in the ceiling are still exposed and Karen asks us to imagine a rope around one of them, a body swinging in mid-air like a large, floppy doll, and the horror of seeing such a thing right before your eyes. "The worker ran around to the door and went into the room, but the hanging man was gone. No dead man, no rope. As you'd expect, this shook the worker up terribly and he started to ask questions. Several days later he found a foreman with some answers."

According to Karen, the foreman, probably Michael Gourley himself, told the worker a disturbing story, one that a lighthouse keeper had told him several years before, back when the light still had a keeper. One day a mysterious stranger appeared at the lighthouse. It seemed that he must have come up from the beach. No one knew exactly from where, or even how he had arrived. He wandered around the property looking as though he were searching for something. Then he went into the house and hanged himself.

"This all happened back in the 1930s," Karen affirms. "That's all the lighthouse keeper knew. That and the fact that since that first sighting, several people had seen the figure of a man hanging in the room."

The lighthouse keeper added that there were other unusual things that continued to happen at the lighthouse during his tour of duty. At night he was haunted by the sound of footsteps coming from behind him as he walked between his house and the tower. "The keeper used to say, the sound of footsteps just kept crunchin' in the gravel," Karen shudders. "And it always gave him the creeps."

From footsteps in the gravel to phantoms in the basement, at St. Augustine Lighthouse the supernatural seems to lurk in every corner. We bid Karen goodbye at the keeper's dwelling and begin our trudge to the top of the lighthouse tower where we have a date with another young woman, with yet another unsettling story to tell.

On our way up the stairs we run into someone else—quite literally run into her because of the narrow passageway. She's the operator of a private tour company in town called Tour St. Augustine, and this won't be the last time we will meet up with Sandy Craig. But on this encounter, Sandy is full of excitement and energy, talking fast like a person with so much to say and so little time. People love her tours and you can see why. Her enthusiasm is contagious.

It happens that she's conducting a tour at that very moment, and she permits us to eavesdrop. "Staff and even some visitors have seen a gentleman up here, way up on the balcony where the light is," she tells her tour group. "They refer to him as 'the Lightkeeper.' This isn't so unusual except for the fact that these sightings are at times when there is no one here. And of course, there is no longer a lightkeeper at this beacon anyway."

"If someone tells us this once, we think, well maybe it's true—but when we hear it so many times, and it's always the same story, we start believing. That's the case with the sightings of 'the Lightkeeper.' We hear about him over and over again. So there must be something to it, don't you think?" She looks around and everyone nods agreeably. Sandy guides her group past us, down the twisting stairway, and we head up to meet Kathleen Steward.

Pretty and self-assured, Kathleen is a former lighthouse guide who says she really enjoys returning to the lighthouse to relive her memories, even though some of the recollections are a little disturbing. Her dark eyes flash expressively. I think she can tell this group is ready to be disturbed.

Kathleen remembers a hot, steamy morning two summers ago. She arrived at work just after daybreak, pulled her car into the deserted employee parking lot, and thought to herself, *first to arrive as usual.* She turned off her engine, opened the car's door, and glanced at the top of the lighthouse.

That's funny, she thought. *Looks like I'm not the first one here after all.* She shook her head, blinked her eyes, and gazed up at the tower again. *Wait a minute, what's going on?*

"Here I was looking up at a man leaning over the railing," Kathleen tells us. "He was standing just to the left of the topside door. No way that was possible."

Immediately she knew there was something terribly wrong. The ground floor entrance door was locked from the outside just as she thought it would be. *No one could be up there—no one,* she said to herself. She hesitated. It was still early and no other staff members had arrived at the lighthouse. Kathleen knew she was alone. Pacing around on the grass below the tower, she'd glance up at the top every few seconds, then back toward the locked door. Was this man the lightkeeper Sandy Craig had mentioned?

Kathleen continued to watch the door. No one had come down so he must still be up top. Finally she made a decision, what she now calls an impulsive one. Running over to the heavy steel door, she unlocked it and started racing up the stairs.

"What did I find when I got to the top?" she asks us. She offers the answer before we have a chance say a word. "Nothing. Not a soul was up there. At least not a living one. Whoever I saw up here was gone." Her eyes narrow, she shakes her head slowly and we know better than to challenge her. She has no doubt about who, or what, she saw.

"The man was a lighthouse keeper. He was looking out to sea—calmly he was going about his business. He was just doing his job as if I wasn't even there. As far as he was concerned, it was *me* who was invisible."

There's a pause and she looks squarely at us, steadying her gaze. "It was a keeper up there. It was a keeper coming back. You want to call it a ghost? Yeah, I call it a ghost."

Whatever spirit was at play in the lighthouse that summer morning is anybody's guess. Kathleen dashes off before anyone's had a chance to ask her if she and Kathy Fleming had ever compared notes. Were their two ghosts really one and the same?

On her way down the stairs, Kathleen hands us off to a tall good-looking fellow named Shane Highsmith, a lighthouse guide in his early twenties.

And Shane is right out of central casting. Dressed to the nines in a period keeper's uniform, shining from his brass buttons down to his black boots, Shane carries himself with strict military bearing. A little stiff, but his broad smile gives away a warm sense of humor. He shakes our hands firmly as we go around the room blurting out our names and hometowns. It turns out our group is from just about everywhere in the country—someone from as far away as Alaska.

"Welcome to the watchroom!" Shane's voice booms, a rich baritone, and his face beams with a sense of pride. Meeting Shane is probably as close as any of us will ever get to encountering a real lighthouse keeper of long ago.

"The watchroom is a floor below the beacon," he explains. "When the keepers weren't performing maintenance on the light, this is where they stayed." He points to a worn, antique writing desk and a matching built-in cabinet that must have served a long line of keepers. Shane tells us that from the beginning St. Augustine Lighthouse was in the hands of a pair of lighthouse keepers. But in 1955, the Coast Guard automated the light. "We're all that's left," he remarks sadly.

"Since 1955, there have been no keepers assigned here. Even though people occasionally see keepers hanging around," he says. And what better place for him to begin his creepy story.

"Two hundred and twenty-seven cast iron steps twist their way to the top of St. Augustine Lighthouse. Everyday they're mounted by hundreds of visitors, dozens of staff, and something else, something you can't see. It's a phantom keeper," he says, "Strange as it sounds, I know it to be true."

From topside here in the lighthouse, Shane declares that it isn't a fear of heights that crawls under his skin. It's a mystery that gives him the willies.

"We stay up here during the daytime and on into the evening," says Shane, speaking for guides like himself who are stationed in the watchroom to greet visitors.

"A lot of times we hear footsteps coming up and, of course, we think it's a customer. So we get ready to do our thing, our standard greeting. Sure enough, the person never comes to the top of the steps. We walk over to the stairwell, look down, and there's not a soul there."

Following Shane over to the iron rail, we look down and try to imagine what it's like up here on a dark night, footsteps pounding up the metal stairs, echoes of phantom boots bouncing around inside the hollow tower. To hear that every night and then to discover there's really no one on the stairs—no one to be causing all this racket—it would be unnerving. "You betcha," Shane laughs, "and you never get used to it."

"I've been here by myself at night and heard the footsteps many times," he exclaims. "I've actually experienced the lights going out on me on a number of occasions when it's pitch dark up here. It's a spooky feeling when you're up on top of the tower by yourself, in total darkness, listening to footsteps that belong to someone who isn't really there."

Shane shares with us the story about the caretaker who took charge once the light was automated. "Footsteps followed him everywhere, up and down the tower, out the door, across the gravel pathway in the yard, and into the old keeper's dwelling. He never saw anything strange, but he used to complain bitterly about the noise. One day he quit. Couldn't stand it anymore."

Shane makes us an offer, but nobody volunteers. "Take my night-turn duty in the watchroom. See for yourself."

It's time to excuse ourselves. We step through the watchroom door out into the tower, prepared for the 227 stairs leading us back down to earth.

Stepping out into a bright sunny day is a little disconcerting. Ghost stories in daylight? That's the acid test. If it's creepy by day it must be terrifying at night.

At the lighthouse entrance we meet David Lapham, a prominent writer of Florida ghost tales, and a devoted lighthouse buff as well. David is soft-spoken and sincere.

He tells us one theory about who the spirit known as "the lightkeeper" might have been. "About a hundred years ago, a lighthouse keeper was painting the top of the tower, one hand holding his brush, the other gripping the iron railing," he explains.

"He reached too far and, of course, he had no safety equipment."

"He was right up there painting the trim on the northwest corner of the beacon," David points to the red trim on top. "He fell and landed right about here, where I'm standing. Of course, he was killed instantly."

We imagine the keeper splayed on the grass. David suggests the dreadful scene was turned even more grisly by gobs of blood-red paint from the keeper's smashed tin can splattered on the ground around him.

Can you imagine a more sudden and violent death than one resulting from a 161-foot tumble off the top of a lighthouse? A fall like that should almost guarantee you become a ghost.

"I'm sure the spirit of the keeper who fell off the tower is still here," David Lapham agrees. "And in my opinion, he is the ghost who walks across the gravel and mounts the steps. The footsteps in the tower at night are his."

"There was also a man who hanged himself." He refers to the dangling body of the stranger described by Karen Harvey. "I think he is the ghost people see in the basement."

We're starting to make some sense out of this—it's like the *Who's Who* of the next world. We head back to the basement, where David Lapham tells us to look for a member of the lighthouse board who is waiting to tell us her strange tale.

We march down to the basement where Jane Masson is huddled by herself, sitting on a wooden crate in the semi-darkness. She immediately confesses to having a bad case of the willies, as she puts it—what dredging up frightful memories will do to you. Jane's heavy fleece windbreaker and snug turtleneck can't keep the chill out of her voice.

"Actually I've had several . . . " she hesitates, looking for the word, "encounters, I guess you'd call them. I believe anybody who has spent a lot of time here has had a few."

"It's very spooky here in the basement," her blue eyes are like saucers. "Even going in to turn on the alarm, I think, do I have to do this?"

Jane's fear dates back at least two years to a night she was taking inventory in the museum gift shop. An errand called her to the basement. Stopping at the bottom of the stairs, she had the feeling she wasn't alone.

Jane tensed, then she jerked her body around to look behind her. She came face to face with a tall shadowy figure.

"The shadow was definitely large," she recalls. "There was obviously something there—something tangible. I could feel the movement, see the shape. I would say it had to have been a man."

"It just moved very slowly past the doorway where I stood." She was standing in the doorway of the video room, the same place Kathy Fleming reported seeing a large, dark shadow.

Jane squeezes her eyes shut and recalls the incident. "I slowly backed up, turned and sprinted up the stairs. This was the first time I actually saw something I perceived to be a person, until I realized there was no possible way this could be a person."

"I had this accompanying sense of dread all the way through my body."

Someone asks Jane the usual question. *Who or what do you think it was?*

"I would definitely say it was a ghost," Jane declares without hesitation. "I don't know who it was the ghost of, but it had to be a ghost."

Looking around the group, I can see we're all a little shaken by the intensity of Jane's account. On his way out the door, one man sighs. "What in the world is going on around here?"

Of course, none of us has the foggiest notion. And what we don't know at the time is that the creepiest story of all is yet to come.

The unknown can assume many different shapes, from ghoulish to innocent. But what could be more chilling than the figure of a pretty little girl—one who you know has been dead for over a hundred years?

"This has always been a very spiritual place, a very mystical place," says Dan Holiday, who occupied the keeper's house in the 1960s when the Coast Guard had a policy of renting it out to civilians.

Dan is a big man with a bushy mustache and rich, warm laugh. He owns a clothing store in St. Augustine's Old City, living nearby with his family. He meets us upstairs of the lighthouse keeper's quarters where we gather around him in a semicircle. All we're missing is a campfire. Some people find chairs but most of us just plop down on the floor. And we all watch Dan intently. His arms are like rotors. His hands do a dance in the air. Dan is expressive. He has the deep voice of an old-time radio announcer. Dan is a born storyteller.

"I ran a coffee house downtown. That was a big thing back then, in the 1960s. Real popular. Various folksingers performed and we served espresso."

Author interviews Dan Holiday on camera in St. Augustine Lighthouse keeper's house for TV film Haunted Lighthouses, *with crew, Richard Schutte, camera, and David Nowicki, audio.*

"Right here," he points at the corner of what is now one huge room, "this is where I used to sleep. "I lived here for thirty-six dollars a month back in the sixties. That was a cheap deal, even then."

He tells us that, practically speaking, he lived here alone. Or almost alone. Dan had grown to accept the fact that he shared the dwelling—shared it with a little girl.

"She hummed," he remembers. "It was a cute little tune, just like any child would hum while playing by herself, perhaps dressing her dolls."

Other times he tells us he heard her playing with a ball, bouncing it on the floor and giggling. "I knew it was a little girl, I knew she was cute, and I knew she must be a ghost," Dan smiles.

Although she was sometimes heard, she was never seen. Until one day a man named Tony showed up.

"Tony was a fabulous banjo player," Dan recalls. "I booked him to play in my coffee house and he needed a place to crash. So I invited him to come over and stay in my spare room."

A few days after Tony moved in, Dan went out on a fishing trip. When he came back Tony wasted no time tracking him down.

"I had the strangest thing happen to me the other night," Dan remembers Tony saying. Dan interrupts his story here to assure us that he never told Tony or anyone else about a little girl or a ghost in the house. "Not a word!" he contends.

Tony told Dan what had happened. It was warm and muggy in St. Augustine that night, and in the moonlight Tony had strolled from the club to Dan's apartment. He remembers that the moon was full and so bright you could see the humidity hanging in the air like a misty curtain. Reaching the apartment after midnight, he went to bed. But he couldn't sleep. Tony propped himself up with pillows and read a magazine. That's when he first heard the humming. It sounded like a child, he said.

Tony got out of bed and started to follow the sound. *Funny,* he thought, *Dan said he lived alone.* But Tony was determined to get a look at whoever was making this sound.

He followed the faint tune up the old wooden steps into the darkness outside the attic door. A sliver of moonlight from under the door shone on the top step. He used that strip of blue light to find his way to the top. He stopped outside the door. The humming sound was behind it. He twisted the door knob. At first he thought it was locked. But strangely the lock released and he slowly pushed the door open. Tony's eyes popped and he froze like a statue.

"When he opened the door," Dan says softly, "he saw a little girl standing with her back to him. She was looking out the front window. Her little body was washed in moonlight."

Dan remembers that Tony shuddered as he recounted his experience. The girl was very young, no more than about twelve years old. She wore her light brown hair in two long braids. Over a plain blue dress, she wore a crisp, white pinafore. And she was humming.

Tony stood perfectly still, watching her from the top stairs, afraid to enter the room for fear of disturbing her. He can't recall how long he stood there, it might have been a minute, perhaps it was longer. Suddenly, the girl turned her head around toward him and met his stare. Her head twisted around but her body didn't move. She glared at him and he thought he might melt in the intensity of her gaze. Sensing he had disturbed her, he took one step back. That's when she disappeared.

Later he said that the best way to describe the way she looked at him was with pity. "She looked as though she felt sorry for me for having seen her—sorry that she had frightened me."

Tony's gig at Dan's coffee house ended, he moved on to another city, and no one spoke about his experience with the little girl

Ghost of young girl who drowned at St. Augustine Lighthouse, portrayed by actress in TV film Haunted Lighthouses.

again. As far as Dan was concerned, the incident was forgotten. Months passed with nothing out of the ordinary happening. On a few occasions, Dan heard the girl humming. He ignored it. As in the past, he didn't see her.

One night Dan had another house guest, an out-of-towner who had never met Tony and knew nothing about the ghost of a little girl in the house. "The man was asleep in the spare bedroom," explains Dan "He heard a very light tapping on the door. When he opened it, there was a little girl, eyes wide and staring straight at him."

Dan remembers clearly what happened next. The man was shaking so badly he fumbled with his suitcase as he packed. It was the middle of the night and he was packing to leave. He stuttered nervously, telling Dan that the girl he saw was about twelve. She had long braids in her brown hair and she wore a white pinafore and a blank stare. On his way out the door he turned and said one more thing: the girl had the look of the dead.

"He never stepped foot in the house again," laughs Dan, and shakes his head with a big sigh.

Dan Holiday knew there was really no child living in the house. Or, as he says, no *living* child. And there hadn't been one here for many years.

"But I know something tragic once happened to a little girl here," he declares. "And I think part of her never left."

History supports what Dan believes, a tragedy did happen here. In 1873, a lighthouse family was devastated by the death of two young daughters. The girls belonged to the man who built the tower.

Photo by Joseph Schiffbauer

Sisters who drowned at St. Augustine Lighthouse as portrayed by actresses in TV film Haunted Lighthouses. *Girl on left is believed to be a ghost who haunts the keeper's house.*

One day while playing in the surf not too far from shore, the girls were swept into the sea. Days went by before their bodies were recovered. It's believed that they were buried on the lighthouse grounds. The younger of the two girls was twelve years old and had long brown hair.

Just as Dan Holiday says, it's a spiritual place. In fact, many people maintain that St. Augustine Lighthouse is rife with ghosts—ghosts that live in dark shadows under basement stairs; ghosts whose footsteps emerge out of nowhere and disappear into nothingness; ghosts who seem harmless but are sure to send you away with icy cold shivers. And intelligent, sane people claim to see and hear these things.

If you wonder why so many hauntings occur at this otherwise serene and picturesque lighthouse, you're not alone. Everyone wonders—and a few will even swear it's true.

"I believe in ghosts," writer David Lapham told me as we packed up our gear and prepared to leave St. Augustine Lighthouse. I walked out the front door and started down the wood steps of the old keeper's dwelling with this distinguished and rational man walking at my side. And he told me as matter-of-factly as anyone else would chat about the weather.

"I've talked to hundreds of people who believe," he said, "and they all say they have seen ghosts. There's no doubt in my mind that ghosts exist."

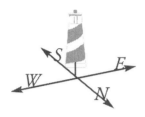

Travel Tips
St. Augustine Lighthouse

This stunning, striped tower looms over the tall palm trees on Anastasia Island, which is across the Bridge of the Lions from the town of St. Augustine.

To reach it from downtown St. Augustine, cross the bridge and head east on Highway A1A, one mile south toward St. Augustine Beach. When you see the black and white lighthouse behind the trees on your left, watch for a left turn onto Lighthouse Avenue. The lighthouse driveway is clearly marked.

The lighthouse is open 9 A.M. to 6 P.M. every day, and there is an admission charge. With easy access from the lighthouse, the museum gift shop is one of the best of its kind.

Park in the gravel lot in front of the keeper's house. I suggest that you have your camera in hand when you begin walking up the path toward the red brick keeper's house with its broad two-story front porch. About halfway, stop and take your first picture. The ancient gnarled oaks, haunting in their own right, frame the classic keeper's dwelling with the bold tower looming behind it. What a shot!

The lighthouse and museum remain open year round. Needless to say, the best time to avoid crowds of tourists and stifling heat is to come in the late fall or early spring. It's very peaceful and everyone seems friendlier, less stressed. Special events are held throughout the year, mainly during the season.

The lighthouse staff gets my award for being attentive and knowledgeable. And that's the way they seem to treat everyone, not just TV people. This facility is a lighthouse lover's dream. If you can visit only one lighthouse, St. Augustine would be a great choice. But hopefully you'll visit a lot of them.

Allow yourself at least two hours to tour the lighthouse and museum, then plan to check out a few other local attractions.

St. Augustine Lighthouse & Museum
81 Lighthouse Avenue
St. Augustine, FL 32080
Daily 9 A.M. to 6 P.M.
Admission Charge
904-829-0745
www.staugustinelighthouse.com

—∞—

Like New Orleans, St. Augustine has preserved the charm and character of its European heritage. In so many ways, it's an exotic place with a foreign flavor. I was reminded of villages in southern Spain with their narrow white-walled alleys decorated with terracotta pots frothing with bright colored flowers, and courtyard gardens hidden behind wrought iron gates.

You might be surprised by the strong emphasis on fine art in St. Augustine. In the sixties, coffee houses were popularized here by a group of self-styled artists known as beatniks. The coffee houses are gone, but remnants of those creative days remain. From the Beat Generation, the town inherited a variety of fine arts galleries and remarkable sculpture gardens.

Some shopkeepers in St. Augustine practice the Spanish custom of mid-afternoon siesta. Shoppers beware, you may have to take a break around two o'clock. You could always honor the custom and grab a quick nap yourself.

Another thing St. Augustine has in common with the Spanish: it's a place that comes to life late at night. One of the more interesting ways to spend an evening in St. Augustine is with Sandy Craig, who operates Tour St. Augustine, a terrific walking tour company.

Predictably, my favorite tour is called *A Ghostly Experience*, and, of course, it only goes out at night. It's a historical and haunting experience. Loquacious guides dressed in period clothing lead you down dark, twisting streets and alleys, lighting the way with crusty old lanterns and satisfying your appetite for tasty tales of mystery and death.

"St. Augustine is a really special place," says tour operator Sandy Craig. "It's unique and mystical, especially at night. That's why we do our ghost tours at night. The city comes alive with the magic of people from way back in the past who have lived here—and, in a spiritual way, some of them still do. Maybe they loved it here so much they decided to hang around."

"This is, without a doubt, Florida's most haunted, maybe even America's most haunted place," she adds.

These walking tours operate daily, there is a charge, and they are highly recommended.

A Ghostly Experience

Call for rates and reservations

888-461-1009

—⁓—

Lightner Museum is located in the heart of the Old City. Built in 1888, by super-rich Henry Flagler as a Spanish Renaissance-style hotel he called the Alcazar, it was bought sixty years later by Otto Lightner to house his vast and varied collections. Today it's home to three floors of fascinating displays—most of them elaborate, some downright eccentric. Overall they call it "Relics of America's Gilded Age."

Steam baths on the second floor offer an intriguing glimpse of the wealthy at play in the late nineteenth century. And Lightner's impressive collection of mechanical musical instruments is demonstrated twice daily in a cacophony of bells and chimes. One room is devoted entirely to Tiffany glass. A regular tour takes about two hours, but you could easily spend half a day here. Highly recommended.

Lightner Museum
King & Cordova Streets
SR A1A (San Marco Ave.)
Daily 9 A.M. to 5 P.M.
Admission charge
904-824-2874

—⁓—

Juan Ponce de León landed somewhere in the area in 1513, in search of the legendary fountain of youth. Alas, he discovered no fountain. But his trip wasn't entirely wasted. He managed to take possession of the region for Spain while he was here. On your way into town on San Marco Avenue, a twenty-five acre archeological park claims to own the *real* thing—Juan Ponce's fountain of youth. If you like your roadside attractions on the touristy side, this may be your cup of tea—or water. During your visit, you'll be offered a not-too-tasty paper cup of water from the fountain itself. If it works, your price of admission was well spent.

Ponce de León's Fountain of Youth
National Archeological Park
11 Magnolia Avenue
Daily 9 A.M. to 5 P.M.
Admission charge
800-356-8222

—∞—

Don't miss the oldest masonry fort in the U.S., the Spanish fortress Castillo de San Marcos. You'll marvel at its bulk. The massive walls, twelve-feet thick at the base, and gun deck holding up to seventy cannons, have seen a lot of action since its construction. It was decommissioned in 1900. Situated on a smooth grassy slope overlooking the blue water, you won't find a more picturesque fort anywhere, or get more exercise walking around one.

If you visit the fort at night, prepare for a possible ghostly encounter. An eerie glow is sometimes seen near a wall in the dungeon that became the ghastly tomb of Señora Dolores Martí in 1784. Her husband chained her to the wall and sealed her inside the room as punishment for her alleged infidelity. Human bones were supposedly discovered here in 1938. Reports of a faint glowing light continue, even today.

Glow or no glow, a visit to the fort is highly recommended.

Castillo de San Marcos National Monument
Castillo Drive & Avenida Menendez
Daily 9 A.M. to 5 P.M.
Admission charge
904-829-6506

—∞—

Hop back on the San Marco Avenue and head for the Old City where you'll discover the true charm of St. Augustine.

The Oldest House Museum is really two museums. One traces the city's history, the other follows the history of Florida's Army from 1565. It's also said to be haunted. Eerie lights have been observed moving in the rooms late at night, even though the house has no electricity. Investigators have never been able to explain what's going on. People experience strange, haunting feelings in here, and even animals become agitated in certain rooms of the house. It was constructed shortly after the British burned the town in 1702.

This museum is a good place to begin your exploration of St. Augustine. Start your tour here and you'll get an overview of the city's rich history with maps and exhibits. Hours are nine to five daily, and there is an admission charge. Recommended.

Oldest House Museum

14 St. Francis Street

St. Augustine, FL 32084

Daily 9 A.M. to 5 P.M.

904-824-2872

—m—

Colee's Carriage Tours have been clip-clopping along the Old City's narrow streets since the 1800s. Call for information or to reserve a horse drawn carriage. Of course, there is a charge for their service and the carriages operate day and night.

Colee's Carriage Tours

Call for rates and reservation

904-829-2818

—∞—

❩ For updated tourist information, call the St. Augustine Visitor's Center (904) 825-1000.

—∞—

🍽 A restaurant not far from the lighthouse on Anastasia Blvd, with a name you're not likely to forget, *Gypsy Cab Co.,* is chef-owned and considers itself *urban cuisine.* Prepare for a wait, but it's worth it. This popular dining spot, decorated outside with purple neon and inside with local art, accepts no reservations. Grouper in tomato basil sauce is a specialty. The salad dressing, a unique spicy herb blend, has become so popular you can buy it by the bottle. Black bean soup is a mainstay, thick and spicy. *Gypsy Cab Co.* serves cocktails, and prices are moderate to expensive. It accepts most credit cards.

Gypsy Cab Co.

828 Anastasia Blvd

A1A 1 mile south of Bridge of Lions

904-824-8244

—∞—

🍴 Not as adventurous as *Gypsy Cab Co.*, but a very good choice nonetheless is the *Columbia Restaurant* on St. George, smack in the center of the Old City. It belongs to a chain of Florida eateries of the same name, but the place has a unique feel to it. The menu features terrific black bean soup with choice of toppings, and a variety of grilled fish. I go for the grouper every time—and that's been many times. Prices lean toward expensive here, but quality is high. They accept reservations, serve cocktails, and honor most credit cards.

Columbia Restaurant

98 St. George (St. George at Hypolita)

Old City

904-824-3341

—⁂—

🍴 For casual dining, a huge seafood menu, and affordable prices, take the family to *Barnacle Bill's Seafood House*. Tourists flock here, but I didn't see many diners who appeared to be locals. That's okay, because the food is fresh and the portions are large, and the kids will love it.

Late one night, after a long day of shooting film at the lighthouse, I treated the crew to a man-sized Barnacle Bill's seafood feast. They're not kids, but they loved it anyway. Shrimp and crab cake dinners all the way around, with clam chowder and Florida gator tail appetizers. It's conveniently located downtown, across from the visitor information center, and on most evenings, you can expect a long line. Cocktails are served and credit cards honored.

Barnacle Bill's Seafood House

14 Castillo Drive

904-824-3663

—⌘—

 More than two dozen Bed & Breakfast inns offer an exciting variety of lodging opportunities in St. Augustine.

Downtown on the bay front is a particularly charming B&B, and it comes with a high recommendation from lighthouse staff. The Casablanca Inn on the bay is a grand white mansion with white porch columns and sprawling verandas. (U.S. Airways named it one of Florida's ten best inns.) At a breakfast meeting prior to our filming at the lighthouse, I enjoyed a gourmet breakfast with fresh fruit and home-baked muffins in the elegant dining room. The sleeping room I saw was small but beautifully furnished with antiques, a large private bath, and a stunning bay view.

As a bonus for ghost buffs, the Casablanca Inn may be haunted, at least that's what I heard from Sandy Craig during my ghost tour. Apparently the place is home to a ghostly lady who appears outside the inn around midnight, up on the widow's walk. She creeps along the high walkway with a lantern, as though she's signaling to someone. The theory is that she used to be the owner of the inn and this is how she helped her rum-running friends enter safely into the harbor. Sandy contends the ghost never bothers guests of the inn, preferring to remain outside on the roof.

While not inexpensive, you'll find some surprisingly affordable packages on their website, www.casablancainn.com.

Casablanca Inn Bed & Breakfast

21 Avenida Menendez

800-826-2626

—〜—

For a complete list of other Inns and B&B's in the area, visit the web site of Historic Inns of St. Augustine, www.staugustineinns.com.

The Eternal Bloodstain
Pensacola Lighthouse

Florida

Lighthouses are a lot like people. Some are more interesting than others. The lighthouse in Pensacola, Florida, is a gem—historic, mysterious, and haunted.

Who can fathom why so many people consider Florida America's most haunted state? Is it Florida's long, mysterious history? After all, St. Augustine, on the east coast, is America's oldest city and reputedly host to a whole gallery of ghosts.

Does it have something to do with all the water surrounding Florida? Some people believe spirits are attracted to water—even empowered by it. Water is everywhere here—wetlands, swamps, springs, bays, lakes—wherever you look, there's bound to be water. If it's true that spirits percolate in water, the Florida peninsula is surely one of the most ghost-infested regions of America.

Ghosts of headstrong people have a way of returning to their old stomping grounds—or so some people will tell you. That's another explanation for Florida's reputation as a ghost haven. Throughout history, the state has seen the most colorful cast of characters imaginable traipse across its stage. Interestingly, many of these characters seem to have remained—even after death.

"The hundreds of miles of coastline here have seen a long and bloody history," says Florida writer Lee Holloway. "Pirates have romped all over Florida, ships have gone down by the score, battles have raged, from the early Spanish to the American Civil War. Florida probably has more buried treasure than any other state. Wouldn't you expect a few ghosts to go along with it?"

Florida is highly spirited, indeed—in every sense of the word. Where else can you find the restless ghosts of pirates, conquistadors, gangsters, Native Americans, and sea captains all intermingling?

Photo by Gordon Levi.

Pensacola Lighthouse is a charming place, but it harbors a darker side, and some say a bloodstain that cannot be washed away.

And with the existence of ghosts *and* seacoast, you're bound to stumble on haunted lighthouses.

In the previous chapter, St. Augustine Lighthouse turned out to be a place where every dark corner and hidden cranny seemed to harbor a ghost. Now we're headed west, to the other side of the state, to a lighthouse that appears no less haunted than its east coast kin, and perhaps even more mysterious.

Deep in the state's panhandle—as far as you can go before you venture into neighboring Alabama—you'll discover Pensacola Lighthouse, a tall, handsome beacon with a distinguished air about it. It's everything you'd expect from a lighthouse situated on a military base—the Naval Air Station at Pensacola.

The 150-foot conical brick tower is painted white on its bottom third and black on its top two thirds. The lantern at the top is painted black, completing the overall formally dressed appearance. Black and white against a sky of azure blue make a very dramatic statement. And the history here has a dramatic side as well.

Nestled beneath the lighthouse is a large, white two-story keeper's dwelling. In this region, roofed porches are often called verandas, from the Portuguese meaning balcony, and the high, wide veranda spanning the entire width of this house is worthy of such a romantic term. One can imagine visiting here in simpler times, spending long sultry evenings sipping sweet tea, catching up on the latest happenings, perhaps even swapping a few good ghost stories.

It's a place to gaze at the stars and listen to the pounding surf, giving you a little spiritual rush, like you're communing with the universe. And you may get a sense that you're not the first person to have done that here. As a matter of fact, many generations have shared this view of the heavens—mostly lighthouse families, coming and going, some blessed by happiness, others dogged by tragedy. Lives have started here, lives have ended, and pieces have been left behind.

Pensacola Lighthouse is an enchanting place, but it harbors a darker side. Spend some time inside the tower, or in the keeper's dwelling, and the spiritual feeling you experience might be a disturbing one—as if certain forces here are not at peace. Have you disturbed them? Are those eyes watching you from a darkened corner, or is it just your imagination? Is that shiver in your spine from a draft, or a nagging fear of the unknown?

You may have heard stories about another old building on the base nearby the lighthouse, a former hospital that's reported to be haunted. Some go so far as to say it's hopelessly infested with phantoms. Workers on the base in the old days whispered about the eerie sounds they heard and menacing wraithlike figures they saw hiding in the stairwells.

More recently, after the hospital building was converted to offices, staffers witnessed objects flying across the room, doors opening and slamming shut on their own, and lights flickering mysteriously. One office worker found ghostly writing on the walls, too high up in the corners for a person to reach. The writing declared, "Death Awaits," and a simple "Help." The strange scribbling was never explained.

The hospital was built in 1826, but it was two years earlier that the intriguing history of the lighthouse began.

After the U.S. purchased Florida from Spain, it didn't take the government long to recognize the importance of Pensacola Bay as a perfect site for a Naval base. Local officials were anxious to make the bay safe for ship navigation, so in just months, construction of a lighthouse was authorized. Pensacola was about to become the first lighthouse site on the Gulf Coast.

The perfect location, a forty-foot hill just west of an ancient Spanish fortress, was chosen. The walls of the structure, Fort Barrancas, were still standing at the time—they do not exist today. Strangely, the new site was smack on top of the old fort's cemetery. What was done with the graves is anyone's guess.

"A cemetery was always built on the highest point of ground. Why? We don't really know," explains Lee Holloway, who has spent years researching the light and its history. "Something to do with it begin closer to the gods, maybe."

"We know why a lighthouse is built on a rise. It means in order to reach a certain height you need to build less lighthouse. Costs go way down. But this may not have been the best place to locate the lighthouse. Bodies were disturbed and as a result, quite literally, the remains may have come back to haunt us all."

"Few people know about the technique employed to move a

cemetery. Graves are moved with one shovel of earth. But not the body or remaining bones. There are a lot of questions about this practice, and a lot of superstitions connected to it."

On December 20, 1826, less than two years after it was authorized, the first lighthouse at Pensacola, and the fourth lighthouse in Florida, was lit. It had cost a whopping $6000. Unfortunately, most mariners thought any amount was too much money for something so useless. Complaints started to flood in as soon as the light came on. The tower was not tall enough, trees on a nearby island obscured its beacon, and the light was not sufficiently bright for such a critical location. Heads must have rolled.

In 1859, a second lighthouse replaced the unpopular original. This time there were no arguments about size and stature. It was an impressive structure made more imposing by its location high on a sandy ridge. The tower rose to a lofty height of 191 feet above the sea, and the first-order lens made in Paris, France, was one of the largest anywhere. It flashed a powerful white light every twenty seconds, just as it does today.

To the casual observer, Pensacola Lighthouse looks like many other beacons of its kind on the American coast. In fact, it appears to be a model lighthouse: lofty and noble, strong and reliable. But below the surface, this lighthouse is far from normal. Hidden somewhere in its intriguingly dark history, an explanation for its hauntings must linger—but no one knows where that explanation lies. And nobody has clue about what it might be. It's a mystery and a legend.

The legend is particularly grisly—one that may have been passed down through generations right here on the veranda of the keeper's house. It centers upon an early keeper of Pensacola Light, a man named Jeremiah Ingraham.

Despite suffering a barrage of criticism about the beacon's shortcomings, Ingraham took his position as keeper most seriously. Every two hours he doggedly trudged from the keeper's quarters at the base of the tower to the watchroom at its top—166 steps in all. Slung over each arm he carried a bucket of whale oil to refuel the lamps. It was backbreaking work, and after fourteen years on the job, he died. Some people will tell you it wasn't a broken back that killed him, or a failed heart. They speak about something more sinister that did him in—murder, in fact. His death remains one of the great mysteries hanging over the light, but it isn't the only one.

Something terribly evil happened here on a foul night when the wind blew at near hurricane strength, howling up through the brick tower with such ferocity it sounded like an angry chorus of restless souls. The rain lashed at the windows like razors, beating on the roof like rapid gunfire.

The raw fury of this night was not reserved for the weather outside. Inside, too, a tempest was brewing. While the storm battered the lighthouse tower, the keeper and a woman we believe was his wife, were lashing out at one another. They screamed and cursed in the fiercest imaginable argument, nearly outdoing the intensity of the storm.

Some accounts quote witnesses who remember the fracas. The husband and wife brawled for the better part of an hour. They fought like devils. The fight ended abruptly. Whimpers were heard, then bursts of hideous screams, more like cries of pain than anger. Over and over the keeper shouted, "No! No!"— until finally there was silence. No sound was heard but the wind whipping and rain pelting.

For a moment the house was still—eerily quiet. Suddenly the keeper's wife burst through the front door, dashed out into the lawn, and ran around the yard in senseless circles. All the while she was sobbing uncontrollably. And she was covered with blood. Her arms were streaked with fresh blood, her dress and shoes soaked with dark crimson. Even the water from her rain-soaked hair ran red across her shoulders. In her hands she grasped the ivory handle of a long-bladed fisherman's knife—it, too, dripping blood. She held it high in the air and pointed it at her chest. But seconds before she could impale herself, a passerby wrenched the knife from her deathlike grip and tossed it into the grass.

When the authorities arrived, they restrained the woman and carried her away. All the while she continued her venomous howling.

It wasn't long before the lifeless keeper was discovered in the upstairs bedroom. His half-naked body was draped over the blood-soaked sheets. A glistening stream of red ran from his wounded torso and flowed toward the fireplace, collecting in a pool. Steam from the warm blood rose off the cool pinewood floor, causing a sickening stench in the room.

Self-defense was what the woman pleaded. Though town officials were suspicious of her motives, not to mention the awful violence of her act, they released her to return home to the keeper's dwelling. No one can say where she lay down to sleep that night, or if she slept at all. But by dawn she was up performing the dead keeper's duties, climbing the steep stairs, filling the lamps with oil, trimming the wicks, lighting the light.

The woman's true identity has been lost to history. Most people believe she was Jeremiah Ingraham's wife, others have hinted it was actually his jealous mistress. Whether it was even Ingraham who died in that puddle of blood, we really can't be certain. Nor can we determine whether it was a crime of passion or a case of self-defense. Speculation is all we have—speculation and a persistent bloodstain.

"This so-called crime was committed over 150 years ago," says Lee Holloway, "and all we know is what's been passed down by word of mouth. Newspaper accounts have not survived. But there's little doubt that someone was killed in that room, probably Jeremiah Ingraham. A bloodstain that won't go away is all we have left of a seemingly violent crime."

Although many questions nag at us about this mysterious incident, one gruesome fact is undisputed. The bedroom was someone's death chamber—presumably the keeper's. The sickening bloodstain, seemingly sealed forever in the pinewood floor of the room, marks the spot where fresh blood pooled on that violent night over a century and a half ago. The stain has persisted, and no one has been able to wash it away.

"The stains are definitely blood," Leo Glenn, a local construction worker, told the *Pensacola News Journal* in 1995. "One dark splotch, about a foot in length, lies to the left of the fireplace, while a quarter-size splatter lies to the right, with more splatters across the room. We figured there was a bed here in the middle and they fought all the way around it."

Countless reports and investigations support the fact that a dark stain remains on the floor near the fireplace, stubbornly refusing to budge no matter how hard it's scrubbed or how much it's sanded. Dick Callaway, cultural resource manager for the Pensacola Air Station, firmly believes the stains are blood. He has recorded at least a dozen mysterious incidents involving a crew of construction workers at the lighthouse. These men have reportedly heard laughing, moaning, breathing, and footsteps on the iron stairway. Two of the workers spied a ghostly figure in the window of the locked lighthouse. "Every incident that I recorded had two or more people witness it," says Callaway.

Emmett Hatten grew up at the lighthouse in the early 1930s when his father was keeper. Shane Carter, president of the Southern States Ghost Research Society, states firmly that the stain cannot be removed and he cites Emmett Hatten as his source of information. "He recalls his mother scrubbing and scrubbing that spot to no avail," says Shane. "He also heard footsteps on the iron stairs of the tower at night and human breathing, although no one was inside the tower at the time."

"Emmett Hatten claims that his mother got on her hands and knees and scrubbed with every cleaning agent on the market," reports Lee Holloway. "Each time she thought she had removed the stain. But as soon as the floor dried, the stain reappeared."

Over the years, several visitors to the lighthouse have commented on a strange odor in the bedroom. They can actually smell blood in the room. In a letter, one visitor spoke for the group with which she was touring. "We walked into the room and stood frozen in our tracks. No one moved an inch. The metallic smell of fresh blood practically knocked us over," wrote the woman, who went on to say she and her friends from Georgia were quite shaken by the incident.

Lee Holloway reports Emmett Hatten told her that when he was growing up, the room had strange feelings connected to it. "Emmett said it felt like something or someone else was in there with you. He couldn't explain it. No one can. I've seen the bloodstain myself. It's definitely there—and it's weird."

Shane Carter investigated some of the strange feelings people have reported, and he believes the room has a powerful spiritual presence stemming from the murdered keeper, or perhaps other unidentified keepers who have died in that bedroom of unknown causes.

"If you go to the lighthouse you may run into an eyewitness," Shane reports after his visit to the Naval Base. "I easily tracked one down. Delanee Pullen, a very level-headed and well educated woman who went to the lighthouse one night with her husband, Chief Rick Pullen of the U.S. Coast Guard."

On this moonless winter night, the light in the beacon was not operating. The Pullens volunteered to check on the lighthouse, according to Shane. Chief Pullen unlocked the tower and they entered.

"Someone was inside cussing furiously," Shane Carter reports the couple telling him. "It scared them half to death. They knew nobody could be in there since the door was locked from the outside. But they went in to investigate anyway. No one was inside the lighthouse. No one was anywhere near it."

Shane says Delanee Pullen believes the angry spirit they encountered belongs to a former lighthouse keeper. According to her, he was handling the crisis in his own way. After all, with the light out he would have had to climb all 166 steps hauling a couple of buckets of whale oil before he could relight the lantern. His spirit may have been reenacting a chore he'd done a thousand times during his lifetime.

In another incident, on his first visit to the United States, a Dutch veterinarian was permitted to take his lodging in the keeper's cottage. Apparently, the man was the friend of someone important, and the privilege had been arranged for him. On the first evening of his stay, after a day of sightseeing and a late dinner, he drifted off to sleep. In the middle of the night, he awoke to the sound of someone knocking on his door. When he opened it there wasn't a soul there.

Photo by Gordon Levi

*A passageway at the base of the tower leading to cast-iron stairs
where ghostly footsteps have echoed.*

He was about to return to bed when there came a loud crash from the living room. He ran downstairs and found everything in order, but on his way back upstairs, he felt a strong, cold breeze move past him and rush out of the bedroom. He crept back in, afraid of what he might find. All his belongings were exactly where he had left them—except his belt. It had been carefully removed from the belt loops of his trousers and was missing. The veterinarian hurriedly packed and departed, and never returned to the lighthouse. His belt had mysteriously disappeared and was never found.

On another night, a staff engineer arrived at the lighthouse to perform a routine maintenance check. Unlocking the door and entering, he heard eerie laughter at the top of the tower. It sounded like a madman. The engineer knew there was no other person in the lighthouse that night, but the sound continued as he climbed the stairs. When he was about halfway up the inside of the tower, the laughing grew more and more hysterical, and the engineer more frightened. He decided to go for help and started to back down the steps. In his fright, he fell down a flight of stairs and twisted his ankle. Somehow he managed to crawl out of the tower. He returned later with two sentries, but the noise had ceased and the lighthouse was empty.

In his report, a U.S. Coast Guard captain who had witnessed many bizarre, unexplained events concluded, "This is a strange place."

Dianne Levi, local historian and volunteer at the Pensacola Lighthouse, has reached the same conclusion. "The east cellar of the keeper's quarters seems to have a ghost," reports Dianne. "The strangest things have happened down there," she says with a shudder.

She recalls one incident involving a mysterious rope. For years this rope had been tightly wound around a pipe that runs along the ceiling at the foot of the cellar stairs. Workmen had tried to unwind it, but the rope was permanently calcified to the pipe. One morning during the 1994 lighthouse renovation, a construction crew discovered the same rope in another part of the lighthouse altogether, this time draped over a different set of pipes. To one of the workers it appeared like "a hangman's noose."

"It's a mystery," says Dianne. "And we've always wondered who was responsible. The building was locked when the crew left and no one else had access to the lighthouse. It really made the workmen start believing in ghosts."

The same construction crew was also plagued by continually swinging doors—doors that mysteriously opened on their own even though they were locked.

"After a couple of weeks of putting up with these unnerving episodes, Leo Glenn, the construction supervisor, finally propped a board against the door to keep it closed," explains Dianne. And they weren't the only people to have trouble with the doors.

Dianne remembers hearing about a former caretaker who diligently locked all the doors of the keeper's quarters at night. In the morning all the doors would be unlocked, standing wide open. No one else had keys. The poor man was baffled, but he continued to lock the doors every night, knowing they'd be unlocked in the morning.

"Leo Glenn's daughter, Victoria, used to hear doors inside the keeper's quarters slam loudly after the building was closed for the night," says Dianne. It was Victoria's theory that the lighthouse ghosts were unhappy about the disruption caused by all the construction work. Apparently ghosts don't like change.

Lee Holloway tells a story she heard from a Coast Guard captain who once conducted tours of the lighthouse and keeper's dwelling. One day his wife complained that he had never taken her on a tour. That very night he led her up the steps to the top of the tower. They enjoyed the view and everything seemed perfectly normal until they started walking down.

"The captain was real clear about this next part," Lee said. "The experience really spooked the two of them. 'We heard the hatch slam shut, then the sound of footsteps coming down after us,' he told me. 'We quickened our pace and got out of there in a hurry. But we knew there was no one else in the lighthouse that night.'"

"He drew the line at calling what they had heard a ghost," Lee says. "He just told me, 'I'll only say we heard noises we can't explain.'"

Lee shared another story about unexplained sounds in the tower. Several years ago, two Navy journalists spent a night in the watchroom. They later said nothing could make them repeat the restless night they endured there.

"We were up all night with metal doors slamming and other

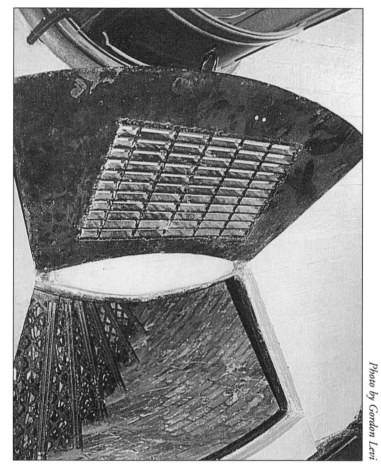

The iron hatch trapdoor, as seen from the lantern room above, which was slammed shut by unseen hands.

Photo by Gordon Levi

clanking noises that sounded like people coming and going," Lee says one of them remarked.

"When they finally got up the nerve to check, of course no one was there," she adds.

This final bizarre incident might be called the last straw for the

U.S. Navy. Immediately after it happened, the Navy formally declared Pensacola Lighthouse haunted. Of course, we knew that already, but now it's official.

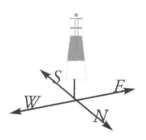

Travel Tips
Pensacola Lighthouse

Pensacola is located on the western edge of Florida's panhandle. It seems like a separate state and state of mind—in climate, geography, even culture. Over here it's more like Alabama than the south Florida beach resorts tourists flock to.

Pensacola proper is skewered by Interstate 10, and finding the Naval Air Station from the highway couldn't be easier. (Enter through the gate on Radford Road.) Gaining entry to the lighthouse interior is not so simple. Although the base is open to the public daily, tours of the tower are currently by appointment only. In the summer season the lighthouse is open on Sunday afternoons, noon to 5 P.M. You can drive around it and explore the grounds anytime the base is open.

Despite its location on the Naval Air Station, Pensacola Lighthouse is maintained by the U.S. Coast Guard, so to make an inquiry, that's who you contact.

The climb to the top of Pensacola Lighthouse is more challenging than many of the other towers we've visited. Unlike St. Augustine Lighthouse, there are no landings to use to catch your breath. Here you'll face 178 steps all at once as they spiral up the tower. But the view is worth the trudge. Imagine as you stand at the iron-railed balcony that this point of light is visible for twenty-seven miles.

Look around and see that we really haven't come that far from the romantic days of oil lamps and lighthouses maintained by uniformed keepers. Pensacola Lighthouse wasn't electrified until 1939, and it was manned as recently as 1965.

Pensacola Lighthouse
Coast Guard Station
Two Way Street, Naval Air Station
Pensacola, FL

—◊—

Although we did not film this lighthouse for a segment of the original *Haunted Lighthouses* TV show, our network location scout was assigned here for three days and turned up some interesting information. It's worth mentioning a few of the attractions you'll discover in Pensacola and the panhandle region. (I hope to include the Pensacola Lighthouse in a future program about more haunted lighthouses.)

While you're here, check out some fascinating exhibits at the National Museum of Naval Aviation, one of the world's largest air and space museums. It displays the first plane to cross the Atlantic.

National Museum of Naval Aviation

Pensacola Naval Air Station

800-327-5002

www.naval-air.org

—m—

In this chapter I've referred to the western panhandle as remote. It wasn't too long ago that this region was pretty wild and woolly, but that's no longer the case. Hordes of vacationers have discovered the charms of Florida's panhandle. Destin, one of Florida's resort boom-towns, is only about twenty-five miles or so from Pensacola. Destin boasts a couple of three-diamond properties and at least one four-star restaurant. It's an easy drive from there over to the lighthouse.

Destin Chamber of Commerce

www.destin-vacations.com

Phantom Footfalls
St. Simons Island Lighthouse

Georgia

Locals may tell you the lighthouse on St. Simons Island is haunted. But no one knows by what. Is it a phantom on the staircase—or just a history of bad luck?

The lofty white lighthouse on St. Simons Island rises magnificently a hundred feet above the lush Georgia Coast. But the beauty of this beacon doesn't betray a gruesome day in its past.

The first tower on this Georgia sea island was erected in 1807. It was a harbor light located just east of Brunswick, designed to serve as an aid to navigation in St. Simons Sound. To save money, most of the material used in its construction was tabby—a mixture of oyster shell, lime, sand, and water. Many locals thought the chalky white tower had a ghostly appearance. It was a plain—some folks called it homely—octagonal pyramid, and so pale that it almost disappeared at certain times of day against the colorless sky. But its beacon served a purpose, and it served for half a century.

The region prospered, ship traffic increased, and a more powerful lens was installed, increasing the station's maritime status to coastal light. But it wasn't long before the hardships of the Civil War threatened to disrupt life on St. Simons Island—including life at the peaceful little lighthouse.

In April 1861, President Lincoln ordered a blockade of all Southern ports. Union warships chased Confederate blockade runners up and down the Georgia coast. In February 1862, General Robert E. Lee ordered the military evacuation of the entire Brunswick area, including the sea islands. But before the Confederates packed up to leave, they had a nasty piece of business to perform. The rebels swept across the island and blew up the lighthouse, rendering it useless to either side.

U.S. Coast Guard photo

St. Simons Island Lighthouse, St. Simons Island, Georgia

For the next ten years, an ordinary cotton barn replaced the beacon, serving as a strange navigational reference for ships entering the harbor.

After the war, a new lighthouse was built on St. Simons Island, topped off about the same time as the tower at Cape Hatteras, North Carolina, the more majestic beacon to the north. That's not to say St. Simons Light made a shabby debut—just more modest. In its own right, this beacon is a picturesque and enchanting place.

"This is a beautiful lighthouse. I think it's one of the most beautiful in America," exclaims Linda King, director of the facility. "It was designed by a very famous architect, Charles Cluskey, who was noted for his Greek Revival style. When you stand facing the keeper's dwelling, your eye is almost magically drawn to the very top. Every architectural element in the structure is designed to lead your eye to the beacon."

But Cluskey never had a chance to see his lighthouse finished. He died at the site before his work was completed. And many of the men on his crew died as well. Even the man sent in after Cluskey to take charge of the project was a victim—but of what, nobody knew. It was a highly contagious disease attacking the island's population with a vengeance. Was it the plague? The fact that it was so mysterious made it that much more frightening.

In desperation, some locals suggested an unseen and unexplained force was responsible. The more superstitious among them thought it might be some supernatural power connected to the old lighthouse—and the fact that it had been disturbed. Spirits don't like change—they get angry.

But the disease turned out to be malaria, a sickness few people understood in those days. It was easier for them to believe in evil spirits. After all, for many years there had been some well-known spirits from the other world rattling around the island. Mary the Wanderer was already loose on St. Simons. All the locals knew the story of Mary.

In life, Mary was a beautiful, petite young girl of about seventeen who lived in a decrepit shack on the island. Her family was poor, but she had always hoped to do better for herself. Sure enough she caught the eye of a fine young man from a wealthy mainland family. They soon fell in love, but circumstances forced them to meet secretly on a lonely little beach near the lighthouse. Then one night, over his father's strong objections, the young man proposed to Mary. He promised to return to the island the next night so he and Mary could run off and get married.

The following evening she rushed to the beach holding a tin lantern—their pre-arranged signal. She waited and waited, waving her lantern frantically, but there was no sign of her lover. Finally she discovered his capsized boat on the island's rocky south beach. Grief-stricken, Mary cast herself into the water and she, too, perished in the sea.

But Mary didn't really leave at all. She returns regularly from her watery grave. For nearly two centuries, a small, frail figure wearing a white shroud and clutching a tin lantern has been seen wandering the shore just south of the lighthouse, still watching and waiting for her lover.

"Mary has been seen too many times by so many people—there has to be something to it," a village merchant and part-time historian told me over coffee at his shop. "I've known people who have seen her. They stop their cars and she just walks right past and down the beach until she disappears. She's been described as wearing white—always a white shroud or veil—and she carries a lantern."

"Come visit here in the fall, the season she seems to prefer, on a moonless night. You just might see her. You might catch a glimpse of Mary the Wanderer herself."

Another story the locals like to tell takes place in a tiny country churchyard, not too far from the lighthouse. Tucked behind Christ Church is a small, gated cemetery with dark green moss creeping across the ground, invading the musty graves and smothering the weathered headstones. This cemetery is haunted, the locals will tell you, haunted by a light—the flickering glow of a burning candle.

For her entire life—and it was a long, good life—a certain woman, a native of St. Simons, was deathly afraid of the dark. Every night, from childhood well into old age, the woman kept a candle burning to chase away the dreaded darkness. When an illness left her too weak to light candles on her own, the woman's husband lit them for her. When she died and was buried in Christ Church Cemetery, her husband visited her grave each night and lit a candle on her gravestone. And when he died, a candle continued to be lit every night, lighting her grave in a warm glow. Of course, no one knows

In the elegant great room of the Cloister resort hotel on Sea Island, Georgia, the author interviews historian Mary Burdell.

Impact Television Photo

who lights the candles a century and a half after her death.

"People see this light, late at night in the cemetery. It flickers like a candle," explains Mary Burdell, historian and storyteller at the world-famous Cloister on Sea Island. "This is not a ghost that anyone sees moving around. It's not one they hear rattling its chains like something out of a Dickens' novel. This is just a light. But it's pretty spooky when you think about it. Here was a person who was terrified of night, and now she's condemned to a lonely, dark graveyard. Her spirit must be flickering in that candle flame."

Wandering spirits, flickering ghost lights, mysterious supernatural happenings, these things were already in the minds of folks on St. Simons Island. So when talk about a haunted lighthouse started to spread, even before construction was completed, it didn't seem at all far-fetched.

Talk they did, and when the new lighthouse became operational, and illness and death continued to plague the staff and keepers, they talked on and on.

"This station is very unhealthy," recorded an early keeper. He might have added—*And this station is very scary. We don't know what's going on.*

The new beacon was finally completed, officially replacing the original lighthouse destroyed during the Civil War. A light once again burned brightly, but these were still dark days for St. Simons Island Lighthouse. And one day in March 1880 stands out as the darkest day in its history.

Lighthouse Keeper Fred Osborne and his young assistant, John W. Stevens, were acting like hotheads, each one intent on causing the other harm. It wasn't bad enough that they were forced to work together by day, at night they shared a cramped quarters in the keeper's dwelling, practically living on top of one another. But as the local rumor mill saw it, the real problem lay in their mutual love interest. The two men were vying for the attention of a beautiful woman—as fate would have it, she was Keeper Osborne's wife.

"That's what they say happened," notes Linda King, Director of the St. Simons Lighthouse and Museum. "We don't know if it's true or not, but it sure makes a good story."

In the nineteenth century, an attractive woman was often

described as fetching. In every sense, Osborne's lovely, dark-eyed wife was that and more—to men on the island, that is. Most women, on the other hand, dismissed her as a heartbreaker, a flirt bent on winning the attention of every man on St. Simons.

As the story goes, tension had turned the lighthouse into a tinderbox—ready to explode at any moment. All it needed was a spark—a spark that finally came in the shape of an angry fist.

Early one Sunday morning in March, Keeper Osborne and the assistant flew off the front porch into the yard, nose to nose, red-faced and breathless as madmen. A shouting match quickly became a scuffle. Wild jabs were thrown as the men rolled in the grass, first the keeper on top, then his assistant. Their mouths twisted and frothed in rage. Neither of the sweaty bodies was willing to surrender.

All the while Osborne's wife stole timid peaks from parted bedroom curtains. Did she believe that no matter who won the fight, she would have her day?

March 6, 1880, local weekly newspaper, *The Brunswick Advertiser*, reported the incident in graphic detail under the small headline: "Shooting At St. Simons Light House."

> On Sunday morning at about 8:30, an unfortunate occurrence transpired at St. Simons Light House, in which Mr. Fred Osborne was seriously shot by his assistant, Mr. John W. Stevens.
>
> It seems that there had been bad feeling

between these gentlemen for several days, and on Sunday morning they went out into the bushes in front of the house to settle their difficulty. During this interview Stevens threatened to chastise Osborne, when Osborne drew his pistol and ordered him not to advance further, whereupon Stevens went back into the house, took down his double-barreled shot gun (which had been previously loaded with buck shot for deer hunting) and as Osborne advanced along the path near the fence, leading to the gate, Stevens fired, at a distance of ninety-eight feet, hitting him in four places, only one shot, however, taking serious effect. This entered the left side of the abdomen, about three and a half inches from, and on a line about an inch above the umbilicus, passed directly horizontally to the right at least nine inches, where it burrowed in the muscular wall of the abdomen.

Osborne, at this writing, is doing as well as circumstances will admit, suffering very much—will probably recover.

From this account, island readers learned the gory physiological details of the shot, but the real bad news didn't hit the doorsteps in St. Simons until the following week.

Frederick Osborne, who was shot in the

Stevens-Osborne tragedy, an account of which we gave last week, died last Wednesday at 3:30 p.m. His remains were taken to Brunswick and interred in Oak Grove Cemetery.

To its credit, the newspaper refused to take sides in this incident. "Of the merits of the case, or who is to blame in the transaction, we forebear to express ourself." Adding, "It is an affair very much regretted by many friends of both parties."

The assistant keeper surrendered, and he was tried and found not guilty of murder by reason of self-defense. This verdict seems odd given the above account of the crime. Following his acquittal, the assistant seems to have disappeared, perhaps moving on to a new, less stressful occupation. Keeper Osborne's widow also seems to have vanished without a trace. People on the island naturally speculated that the coincidental disappearances were suspicious.

The Brunswick Advertiser went on to report in April 1880, a new keeper, Mr. George Asbell, was appointed to replace Osborne with an assistant, whose name was given as Hoyt. It's clear that Mr. Stevens did not continue serving at the lighthouse. But evidence seems to suggest Mr. Osborne at least has tried to stay on.

Frederick Osborne's body was interred at Oak Grove Cemetery. The whereabouts of his *body* is not disputed. But to this day, some question remains about Osborne's *spirit*. There are those on the island who insist that stubborn old Osborne refuses to leave his post—even in death.

By all accounts sensible, well-respected folks propose that Keeper Osborne's spirit must be hanging around the lighthouse—perhaps to exact revenge or watch over his beloved tower. Why he stays is anybody's guess. And there are any number of locals who venture a few.

"His spirit was angry that he was murdered, particularly on duty at his station," observes Linda King, speaking in her office at the lighthouse. "Following the incident, lighthouse keepers and their families supposedly began hearing footsteps in the tower."

Jeff Cole, U.S. Coast Guard Auxiliary, participates in weekly inspections of St. Simons Island Lighthouse. Jeff and two other auxiliary members regularly check the facility from bottom to top. And it's sometimes what they don't find that puts them on edge.

"There are 129 steps going up and they're metal so you can hear somebody climbing the stairs," Jeff declares, "so we keep waiting and waiting and they never get here. We call out like one of our buddies is coming up and we don't get an answer. Then we hear the wind howling in there. It's kind of scary. It's an eerie feeling."

"The Carl Olaf Svendsons are probably our most famous lighthouse family," notes Linda King. "Mr. Svendson was the head lighthouse keeper for over twenty-seven years. Back then it was still considered an isolated station."

"They had three children. The son, Carol Olaf, Jr., remembers growing up here. He would come by and tell us stories about what is was like to be the son of a lighthouse keeper. He'd tell us about all

U.S. Coast Guard photo

Carl Olaf Svendson, one of the early keepers of St. Simons Lighthouse, with his family. It's said that Mrs. Svendson heard the ghost in the tower.

the legends of St. Simons, but especially the legend of the lighthouse stairway ghost."

"Mr. Svendson, Jr. talks about how his mother heard the ghost.

She heard the footsteps in the tower. She would turn around and think it was her husband coming down from the top of the lighthouse. But it would not be Mr. Svendson. It wouldn't be anybody. No one would be there.

"She was convinced it was a ghost," Linda remarks, with a broad smile and a twinkle of skepticism in her eye. "They also had a dog named Jinx. Jinx would supposedly bark at this non-existent being coming down the stairs. Between the dog and Mrs. Svendson, they were true believers in the ghost."

The story really began when the family moved into the vacant keeper's quarters and discovered the dwelling was not as empty as it appeared.

During one of their first nights on duty at the lighthouse, the keeper's wife was in the kitchen preparing supper while the keeper was in the watchroom up top. The narrow opening that leads from the kitchen into the tower was open. That way she could cook and still keep one eye on the tower where the dark spiral stairway wound up to her husband's station.

The family's dog, Jinx, was sleeping under the warm stove while the keeper's wife whipped up a batch of hot biscuits. It was a warm, cozy scene, but one that was suddenly shattered. The near-deafening sound of heavy footsteps boomed on the cast iron stairs, echoing up and down the tower, crashing like thunder in a low-country storm.

The keeper's wife was horrified. The footsteps sounded huge, unreal. Running to the tower doorway, she discovered the stairs were empty. It was not her husband in the tower. Jinx let out a low growl, then erupted in a barking frenzy. He seemed to see something Mrs. Svendson couldn't, to sense the cause of this hellish racket.

The noise stopped and started several times that night—it returned on many future nights. The family grew accustomed to it. In time, the keeper's assistant was asked to take the night watch alone. He refused and had to be replaced by an assistant who wasn't afraid of ghosts.

As for Jinx, he never went near the tower door again. He'd just whimper and hide whenever the footsteps echoed in the lighthouse. The keeper's wife always swore Jinx was the only one who could see—as well as hear—the phantom of the tower.

The family remained at the lighthouse for nearly twenty-eight years. The strange noises never ceased. In later years, Mrs. Svendson remarked that she had grown so accustomed to the sound, she missed the noises when the family moved away.

Sea Island historian Mary Burdell enjoys telling the story of the mysterious footfalls in the lighthouse. "It's one of my favorites tales," she declares. "That lighthouse keeper who died in the front yard of the keeper's cottage, that's the one who we think walks up and down the lighthouse at night," Mary says. "The ghost has never harmed anyone," she continues, "it just kind of gives you the willies."

Does Linda King, lighthouse director, ever get the willies? She's not telling. "I don't believe in ghosts," she claims. Then she adds: "However, if there is a ghost in this lighthouse, it's a good one."

Linda muses about the ghost as a romantic character. One day, out of the blue, the former director of the lighthouse was love struck. "She had worked here for many years," Linda explains. "One day a reporter dropped by. He was following up a lead about the lighthouse hauntings. She showed him around, a romance blossomed, and today they're married. Was it the spirit that brought them together?"

"I don't know," quips Linda, "but that's how I got my job."

"And it's why we think that the spirit of Mr. Osborne has decided to forgive his assistant for murdering him," she says with a grin. "He's not mad anymore."

Although St. Simons Island Lighthouse has had its share of misfortunes and tragedies, according to Linda, "Only good things happen here now."

If that's the company line at this haunted lighthouse, no one has told Coast Guardsman Jeff Cole. He shudders, "Oh, I think it might be haunted here. It's hard to tell. You'll have to stay up here one night all by yourself to find out."

Yeah, right, Jeff!

Some of the best ghost stories are surprises. They seem to spring out of nowhere. The spookiest tale I heard during our visit to the island came only hours before we started to pack up and leave. The crew and I were grabbing some last-minute shots inside the tower, filming nightscapes from the top of the lighthouse. A friendly lady with a pleasing coastal Georgia accent stopped me in the hallway between the keeper's house and the entrance to the tower stairs. She had been watching us while she took inventory in the little lighthouse gift shop. She decided to answer my question before I had a chance to ask it.

"Yes, I believe there's something here. It has to do with the past coming back to life. And there must be something to it." She keeps her voice low, nearly whispering as though she doesn't want to be overheard. "Too many people have seen or heard or felt the presence of this keeper. The one who got shot in the front yard."

All ears, I dropped what I was doing. She encouraged my interest with a warm smile. Her pink sweatshirt bore a picture of the lighthouse and the color set off her silver-streaked hair. Her heavy tortoise shell frames kept slipping down her nose. She edged closer and spoke even more softly. "A few years ago, a young boy and his family were sitting out on the rocks waiting for the lighthouse to open. It was very early in the morning and the sun was just coming up over the water. They were planning to come in and climb the tower."

Just after opening time, as the family was paying their admission, she greeted them. The father took her aside and told her what his son had seen. The boy had been staring up at the tower, watching the beacon flash brightly then slowly dissolve into the misty morning sky. Suddenly, he called out to his sister. "Look, there's somebody already up in the tower." But when he turned back to look at the lighthouse, the man he had seen was gone. The father called the boy over to speak to the woman. "I saw a man up there. He had on a dark uniform and he wore a hat. I watched him cleaning the glass."

"Does he work here?" the boy asked.

"You have a sense when someone is telling the truth—especially kids," says the gift shop lady. "This one was definitely for real. I told him, no, we don't have a lighthouse keeper here anymore and there wasn't anyone up on the tower early this morning. His eyes widened. "Dad," he gulped, "did I see a ghost?"

Before returning to her chores in the gift shop, the woman related her own experience of a brush with a lighthouse ghost. It was more of a sniff than a brush, actually. "One morning I started to open up the lighthouse," she begins. "In the sitting room I noticed an odor of pipe tobacco—sort of a sweet smell. I was upset. No one was supposed to be in here and especially not someone who was smoking. I left the sitting room to investigate and discovered there wasn't a soul in the building. When I went back to the gift shop, the smell was gone. And yes, I've read that the keeper who was killed out on the lawn was a pipe smoker."

"There are so many good stories here, but the details are elusive." Realizing what she'd just said, she laughs and adds, "But we're talking about *ghosts*. Aren't they supposed to be elusive?"

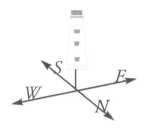

Travel Tips
St. Simons Island Lighthouse

St. Simons Island, one of four barrier islands making up what are known as the Golden Isles of Georgia, can be reached by taking Exit 8 off I-95 to access the Golden Isles Parkway and following SR 17 to St. Simons Causeway, a toll road (approximately fifteen miles from I-95). At the southern tip of the island is the village of St. Simons.

To reach the lighthouse, cross the causeway to King's Way, turn right on Mallory Street, left on Beechview Drive, and right onto 12th Street.

One of only five surviving lighthouses in Georgia, St. Simons Island Lighthouse remains a navigational aid for traffic entering St. Simons Sound. Its powerful lens shines eighteen miles out to sea.

After the tower was destroyed during the Civil War, Georgia's most noted architect and native of Ireland, Charles Cluskey, was hired to rebuild the lighthouse. That was in 1870, and the 104-foot beacon designed by Cluskey is what we see today, with the addition of a lighthouse keeper's dwelling in a unique Victorian design.

The Museum of Coastal History, located in the former keeper's dwelling, displays changing exhibits depicting the history of St. Simons Lighthouse and the rugged lifestyle of the lighthouse keeper and his family.

> St. Simons Lighthouse and the Museum of Coastal History
>
> St. Simons Island, Georgia
>
> Open 10 A.M. to 5 P.M., Monday to Saturday,
>
> and 1:30 to 5 P.M. Sunday
>
> Admission charge
>
> Call 912-638-4666 for holiday hours
>
> and special event schedule.

—◊—

St. Simons Island Visitors Center is located in the village near the lighthouse at 530 Beachview Drive. They can direct you to several worthwhile attractions. Don't miss Fort Frederica National Monument. In 1736, General James Oglethorpe constructed the earthwork that became Fort Frederica, one of the most important forts in America. A small museum displays excavated objects and features a thirty-minute historical film.

—◊—

There is a wide range of lodging accommodations here in the Golden Isles. You have four islands from which to choose, including quaint, out-of-the-way St. Simons, or trendy, upscale Jekyll Island, home of the graciously restored, turn-of-the-century Jekyll Island Club Hotel.

We stayed across the street from the lighthouse at the St. Simons Inn By The Lighthouse. It was convenient and certainly adequate, if a little spartan. We loaded our gear on a two-wheel dolly and pushed it across the street every morning—a rare convenience that gave this inn an extra star in our book.

St. Simons Inn By The Lighthouse
St. Simons Island

—⁂—

An old-fashioned motel people used to call a motor court, The Queen's Court is in the center of the village. Our location scout stayed here and found it clean and reasonably priced. The couple who operate the motel are charming people who know the island backward and forward. We even interviewed them for the TV show.

The Queen's Court Motel
912-638-8459

—⁂—

Is staying in the center of town absolutely essential for you? If not, look around on the fringes. Newer properties such as the Hampton Inn, where we accommodated people who appeared in our television production, were inviting, clean, and affordable—with free breakfast. Great for vacationing families.

Hampton Inn
Demere Road
912-634-2204

—⁓—

If money is no object, the Cloister on Sea Island is one of the East Coast's most touted upscale resorts. The Cloister is accessible from St. Simons Island by causeway, a trip of about thirty-five minutes. During the filming of *Haunted Lighthouses*, an interview with one of the Cloister's historians gained us admission to an otherwise secure resort. We didn't see a sleeping room, but we did tour the public areas, which are elegantly furnished, and adorned with stained glass and rich woodwork—even exotic birds. The central great room, where we first set up lights and camera for the interview, was just around the corner from a huge wall of bird cages, floor to ceiling. These beautiful creatures caused a horrible racket, obviously disapproving of this motley crew. We left for a quieter location.

The Cloister

Sea Island, Georgia

800-Sea-Island

www.seaisland.com

—⁓—

Restaurants on the Golden Isles are plentiful, covering all price ranges and cuisines. Casual dress is accepted in all but the most upscale establishments, where we did not dine. As you'd expect, native seafood is featured everywhere.

On St. Simons Island, near the lighthouse, we enjoyed Blanche's Courtyard so much on our first visit, we returned the following night. The restaurant is a little dark for my taste, and the service a bit stiff, but the kitchen does turn out good food. After a tough day of climbing up and down the lighthouse stairs, I particularly enjoyed the large, comfortable lounge outfitted with plush sofas and overstuffed easy chairs. An icy martini didn't hurt.

The grouper with ratatouille and asparagus was a great choice—twice. Prices fall into the moderate to expensive range. Most credit cards are honored.

Blanche's Courtyard

912-638-3030

—⁓—

For dining and ambience, the big winner on St. Simons Island is Rooney's—upscale in every respect, yet cozy and inviting.

We were welcomed for a late dinner in our lighthouse work clothes—jeans and sweatshirts. Red snapper here is done to perfection, and mine was topped with an intriguingly spicy salsa. One of our more adventurous crew ordered the ostrich dinner and he raved. Leaning toward expensive, but worth every penny.

Rooney's

912-638-7097

—₥—

We saved some money by lunching on alternate days at Dresner's Restaurant and the Sandcastle, both in the Village of St. Simons. Take my advice, wherever you go, ask where the locals eat lunch. These places were it. The service in both restaurants is friendly and the food fresh and filling—a real taste of St. Simons Island where natives outnumber tourists for a change.

Dresner's Restaurant and the Sandcastle

Village of St. Simons

America's Most
Haunted Lighthouse
Point Lookout Lighthouse

Maryland

*A ramshackle skeleton of a house with a tin lid stuck on top—that's
what you'll discover here. Faded red shutters, a broken down front porch,
scrubby pines competing with weeds in the yard—it all adds up to a
grim picture of neglect. This is a lighthouse? Where's the tower?*

*But don't be fooled by its humble facade. Approach with care—the
ghosts of Point Lookout may scare you to death.*

To help guide ships safely from the Chesapeake Bay up the Potomac River and to the nation's capital, Point Lookout Lighthouse was erected at the southern tip of Maryland's western shore. The year was 1830. Andrew Jackson had just been elected president. The nation was already torn over the issue of slavery, but it would be another thirty-one years before it would split apart and erupt into the great Civil War.

For three decades, the beacon at Point Lookout served peacefully, isolated from the rest of the state and easily forgotten on this heavily forested peninsula. But when the war came, Point Lookout was no longer lonely, and no longer safe.

As the battles raged, one of the most horrific prison camps conceived by either side was placed on a site near the lighthouse. Point Lookout Prison was intended to hold 10,000 Confederate prisoners. But shortly after it opened, it was already crammed with twice that number.

The prison hospital was also desperately overcrowded. Fifteen spokelike wings jutted out toward the river—each a separate ward overflowing with hundreds of sick and wounded soldiers. Following the Battle of Gettysburg, conditions went from bad to worse with the arrival of more prisoners. Those men who were not wounded suffered their own kind of private hell, enduring a host of dreadful diseases: typhoid, scurvy, dysentery, and smallpox. People say Point Lookout rivaled Andersonville for its inhumanity.

"Sanitation was very poor here," emphasizes Civil War historian

Point Lookout Lighthouse, Point Lookout, Maryland, has been called America's most haunted lighthouse

Susan Youhn, an expert in Point Lookout Prison Camp history. As Susan summons up of the most horrific examples of the prison's failings, she turns her attention to a swampy stretch of mosquito breeding ground about twenty yards from the river bank.

"Gangrene was probably the biggest threat—it would have necessitated amputation. Limbs were probably disposed of near the lighthouse, dumped right here in this bog," she shudders. Today it's not amputated limbs that litter the murky water but dead, twisted tree branches. It might not be advisable to lose your way down here after dark. A splash of moonlight on a gnarled branch can stir the imagination.

Mark Nesbitt, author of *The Ghosts of Gettysburg*, is well known for chasing down spirits on Pennsylvania battlefields. During his visit here in Maryland, Mark explains that he experiences the same eerie feelings that he gets back home. "These men were dying left and right," he declares. In fact, more than three thousand Confederates perished here.

Imagine a place where men caught rats for food as well as sport. A place where captive soldiers feared the only way out was death. In many cases they were right, and given the choice, many preferred to die.

"They had tremendous pain and anxiety." Mark grimaces as though he can sense the pain himself. "Not knowing what was going to happen to them day to day, they were agonizing over their families. They knew the country was in terrible turmoil, and now all they could do was watch their young friends die in pain."

What about the nightmarish noises at Point Lookout? The

sounds must have been as horrible as anything you can imagine, suggests Susan Youhn.

"There would have been a lot of moaning, but otherwise I think it would have been quiet," she says. "I don't want to call it deathly quiet, but most of these men were away from home, they didn't want to be here, they were suffering. They were homesick and depressed."

Parapsychologists theorize that such distress and anguish can lead to spiritual unrest. "I've been to lots of places that are spiritual," Susan sighs. "Places that have an essence of people who left a part of themselves behind. These men did. They left their arms, their legs, in some cases their fighting spirit, right here."

For decades, visitors to Point Lookout Lighthouse have seen and heard more than they bargained for. "I can't imagine a place that would lend itself more to haunting than Point Lookout," says Mark Nesbitt.

"You can practically cut the psychic energy in the air here with a knife," a staff person at the lighthouse tells me. "On ground as spiritually fertile as this, you can just imagine the energy rising up in rippling waves like heat off a hot asphalt road."

Some people come here to bask in this energy, perhaps in an attempt to channel it, or at least in an effort to understand where it's coming from. Michael Humphries is such a person.

Humphries is a man who wears many hats. He is an author, director of a Maryland museum, and a respected lighthouse historian. But his passionate interest in the paranormal is what draws him to Point Lookout. He can't seem to stay away from the place. And he frequently comes prepared—armed with a tape recorder and notebook to study the festering paranormal activity on this unsettled soil. And the lessons he has learned are very disturbing indeed.

"Help me!" cries a disembodied voice. "Help me!" it screams in terror.

A small tape recorder rests on the dusty table inside the abandoned lighthouse quarters. The tape spins on the cassette and the voices emerge one after the other, each one telling a frightful story.

"The spirits are here," says Humphries, gesturing to the room with a sweeping motion. "I believe there are spirits that do not know how to move on, or they have a really close tie that they're afraid to let go of," he explains in his deep, commanding voice.

Michael Humphries has recorded voices in the basement and attic of the lighthouse—voices that might scare the living wits out of you. On the dozen or so tapes he has collected, raspy, indistinct noises are heard, some sounding eerily human.

"When you pick up the tape recorder and hear the voices, after the curiosity wears off, you still have something that many times is a cry for help. So what I try to do is say a prayer for their souls." He punches the recorder's play button and the first tape rolls.

"Please help me!" screams a woman, sounding frightened and desperate.

"This side after death," moans a man in a weak, creaking voice.

Mark Nesbitt of Gettysburg supports Humphries' claim that

these voices are real. Nesbitt even has a name for what's going on. "It's called EVP, Electronic Voice Phenomenon. You don't hear the sound of the voice or words [when you're recording], but they show up on the audio tape or even in the sound portion of a video tape," he says.

Humphries slides another tape into his machine and presses play. "You're on top of me," cries a woman.

"This is my home," barks out another voice, impatiently.

"Get out. Get out." The childlike voice repeats over and over, sometimes growling the words, angry at someone—or everyone.

In what sounds like a short audio clip from a Civil War movie, a man shouts a command. "Fire if they get too close." But this is no movie—it's too real. He repeats the command, breathlessly, more urgently. What is going on here?

No one really knows, Humphries admits. "I don't believe these are just ramblings from outer space. Many times they're so pointed in what they say, the timing is just too perfect. The timing says it all."

Historian T. J. Youhn collaborates with his wife Susan in researching prison life at Point Lookout. "If pain and suffering are things that bring the spirits out, then Point Lookout definitely would be a candidate for the spirits still being here," he says.

When asked if the spirits here are still suffering, or if they will ever find peace, Mark Nesbitt hesitates before he responds. "I don't know. I just don't know." He shakes his head slowly. "One of the most famous farewells that Civil War soldiers would say was: 'See you in hell, Johnny. See you in hell, Yank.' Perhaps Point Lookout is the meeting place and we're the witnesses. To those dead soldiers, this is hell."

If the spirits are stirring at Point Lookout, sounds are just a part of the ghostly mix. If a picture is worth a thousand words, Laura Berg has a mysterious photo that speaks volumes. The photograph, taken in her living room inside the lighthouse, appears to tell two stories. And one of them suggests there's a ghost loose in this crumbling lighthouse.

In the 1980s, Laura Berg worked in a nearby town and rented the lighthouse dwelling. With her cats and collection of books, she called the lighthouse home for nearly two years.

One night a group of her friends gathered in her living room. They met here about once a month for pizza and a little gossip, according to Laura. She recalls that one of the women had a habit of taking pictures with her Polaroid instant camera. On this particular night, the woman was snapping pictures furiously.

Every few minutes another photo was passed around the room. The young women laughed good-naturedly.

Suddenly the laughing stopped. One of the pictures gave them pause. It showed a man standing by the stairs—a man who had not been invited to the party. As a matter of fact, he was someone the women had never seen. At the edge of the frame, he appeared, a hazy figure in the unmistakable jacket, sash, and pants of a Confederate

*A ghostly Civil War soldier mysteriously appeared in a photo taken inside the
Point Lookout keeper's house, as reenacted in the TV film* Haunted Lighthouses.

Civil War officer. They all agreed he was caught on film, but they

were just as sure of something else. Despite his appearance in the

Photo by Joseph Schiffbauer

photograph, this man was not with them in the house. What had been awkward giggles had turned into frightened gasps. No one was comfortable with what they were looking at.

"I was in the room facing the actual corner where the soldier appeared. But there was no soldier standing there," says Laura emphatically. As a matter of fact, there was no soldier anywhere near the lighthouse that night.

The party broke up early. The next day Laura and her friends talked, and they were still disturbed. Deciding to seek another opinion—a professional one—the women went to the state capital. "We took the photo to a historian in Annapolis. He authenticated it, but the man was stumped about how it could have happened. We were told it was a Confederate officer's uniform and that the soldier appeared genuine in every way."

What was a Confederate soldier doing in Laura Berg's living room? Expert Mark Nesbitt has a theory about the photo. "When people witness a ghost, or some sort of paranormal phenomenon, it seems there's a rip in time, a tear in the fabric of time," he comments. "All of a sudden you get a glimpse, and you see something that just can't possibly be, then it closes as quickly as it opened."

Laura Berg calls her brush with the unexplained a trial by fire, like some strange force wanted her out of the house. It wouldn't work. Armed with resolve, she wasn't going to allow anyone or anything to scare her out of this lighthouse. It was her home.

"There are a lot of things that I cannot figure out: Why they happened, how they happened or anything about them," she declares. "I hadn't given ghosts much thought before, but after the first night at Point Lookout, I became a believer."

That's when Laura started a journal. She decided to write down every experience, every feeling, every sound. Page after page of her journal contain references to paranormal activity.

October 3 was a date Laura spent the night alone in the lighthouse, or so she thought:

"Last night I was awakened by a banging in the attic. It was extremely loud and I have no explanation for it. This morning I heard singing next door. Last night I heard various men's voices when I came in."

"I did feel there were soldiers in the house," Laura recalls. "I would hear groups of men talking on the other side of the wall and I felt like they were soldiers. But I knew there were no living beings over there."

Laura searched for answers in her Point Lookout history books. The first lighthouse keeper assigned to this station died before he took command. For thirty years, the job was carried out by his widow, Ann Davis.

"I felt one of the spirits in the house was Ann Davis. I often felt she was standing at the top of the stairs. Some people who visited the house saw her. My mother heard her."

Although Laura's mother never actually saw the ghost, when she visited her daughter's home in the lighthouse, there was someone else present who knew her name. On several occasions, in the middle of the night, a voice echoed through the darkness. "Helen." Her mother's name came from the top of the stairs. "Helen. Helen."

Over and over the voice called to her mother. "Helen. Helen."

"This was a real voice," Laura insists. "We'd both hear it at the same time." The two women would scramble out of bed, turn on lights, and discover there was no one at the top of the stairs. Or anywhere else in the house, for that matter. Except for the two of them, the dwelling was empty.

"Her name would just be spoken," Laura recalls, "not yelled or whispered. It was much like an anxious person repeatedly calling her name."

Looking back, it's hard for Laura to recall these otherworldly events in an orderly fashion. Their mysterious nature gives them a surreal quality—like the details of a dream you try to remember when you first wake up. Laura's diary is some help, but the timing of her strange encounters is sometimes vague. When, for example, did Laura first notice the ghastly odor in the second-floor rear bedroom? It must have been there almost from the beginning, she says.

It was a vicious smell. Laura remembers the day it filled her lungs with noxious air that made her sick. The smell seemed to creep from cracks in the plaster, seep from the back of a dark closet, ooze from under the splitting floorboards. Visitors who sensed it likened the stench to that of decaying meat. One man called it the scent of death itself.

103

Where it came from, no one knows.

"I scrubbed that room from top to bottom," Laura insists. "The smell would always come back."

Can the history of Point Lookout provide us with any clue to help solve the mystery of this room?

Records tell us that during the Civil War, a number of women prisoners were held at Point Lookout. It's likely that these female captives were locked up in the rear bedroom—the room with the horrible odor. It's as far away as possible from where the male prisoners were housed, across the road. A parapsychologist who once visited the lighthouse suggested that such a holding cell for prisoners, in this case women, might retain negative energy they left behind. He characterized the energy as a remnant of extreme pain and anger. This energy may have lingered after the departures or deaths of the prisoners, and it's expressed through the recurring repugnant odor.

And a foul smell isn't all that lingers. A barrage of loud noises comes from this room as well—further evidence for Laura that something unseen and unexplained still dwells here. During the long evenings that she spent alone in the lighthouse, Laura heard muffled human voices coming from behind the room's closed door—sounds of people eating noisily, coughing, and groaning. Sometimes she heard whispers, and evil little chuckles. One night a scraping sound emerged from the room, a noise she identified as furniture being dragged across the floor.

Next morning she expected to see the furniture rearranged. She opened the door to discover nothing had been moved. Ghosts? If so, Laura Berg learned to live with her spiritual housemates—all except one.

"The electricity would go out quite often. It didn't take much, just a windy night. And I had to go down to the basement, to the fuse box." She shivers at the thought of it. "To me that dark cellar was the creepiest part of the house."

"I did see a figure down there," she says. "I could tell the figure was large, almost too big to be human. I would feel somebody staring at the back of my neck. It was just a little bit frightening."

A little frightening, to say the least. The Maryland Committee for Psychical Research came to Point Lookout hoping to document some of these scary reports. In separate newspaper stories published by a local journal called *Enterprise* abut two decades ago, the committee's findings were chronicled.

In one article, Gerry Sword, Park Superintendent, is quoted confirming that Dr. Hans Holzer, famous professor of parapsychology at New York Institute of Technology, led the team of researchers. Holzer is the author of more than sixty books on the paranormal, and was the host of NBC's *In Search Of* in the mid 1970s. The second article was written by Gerry Sword himself.

The group first became interested in Point Lookout after investigating similar paranormal activity at the Gettysburg National Battlefield. There they discovered that many Confederate captives were shipped to the Point Lookout prison camp.

According to the *Enterprise,* Dr. Holzer's team included several trans-mediums. As they moved from room to room the mediums pointed out places where spirits were lurking, in corners of rooms, closets, and dark hallways. One psychic, a woman, felt a young man had been murdered here, that it was the result of a jealous affair, and that the man's spirit was still at large. Someone else had been held in the building against his or her will, said another medium, but no further information about that person could be felt.

At least two more committee visits were arranged for further investigations. Many hours of tape recordings were made at the lighthouse and other areas of the park. About five minutes of unexplained voices and sounds were captured. Gerry Sword reports that the voices were young and old, male and female, sometimes singing, other times cursing, at least twice calling for help.

A voice of an old man cried out, "Get off that pier." A lady calmly said, "Let us take no objections to what they are doing." In a pathetically small voice, the eerie question of a young boy haunted the investigators. The boy simply asked, "Can I play?"

What causes such activity? Gerry Sword's article concludes, "We have walked on the moon but cannot explain what talks and walks among us at Point Lookout. At least not yet."

Upon leaving Point Lookout, Sword reports that Dr. Holzer commented, "That place is haunted as hell."

The mediums felt lingering spirits, Laura Berg saw a dark fig-

U.S. Coast Guard Photo

Point Lookout Lighthouse

ure in her basement—but they're not the only ones who sensed someone who wasn't there.

Donnie Hammett is a twenty-year veteran of the Maryland State Park Police. In uniform, he possesses the kind of affability that was the signature of TV Sheriff Andy Taylor of Mayberry. But behind this friendly facade, Hammett is one tough cop. And when he's on duty at Point Lookout, there's no mistaking who's in charge.

But something happened one warm spring afternoon that melted the tough guy image, and really shook Hammett up.

He was on duty checking the waterside picnic grove when he

Impact Television photo

Point Lookout Park Police officer, Don Hammett,
who experienced a strange encounter with a lady
he suspects was a ghost.

noticed an elderly woman roaming the grounds in the picnic area. She
was a stranger. "She paced around in this grove of trees," he recalls. "I
noticed she was looking down at the ground, parting the grass with
her feet. I thought she had lost something, possibly her car keys."

It was unusually mild for March. That's how Hammett
remembers the frail woman's attire. She was bundled in a dark,

woolen coat that had smudges of dirt and what looked like straw sticking to it. Wrapped tightly around her narrow shoulders was a heavy shawl. Where had she come from to be dressed this way, Hammett wondered.

Without warning, the woman looked up at him. Her face was pale, almost chalky white, and her eyes were at once piercing and empty. She raised her left hand and tried to point with a bent finger that shook so badly her entire body moved with it. Was she cold? Hammett wondered. The woman spoke and her voice, too, was frigid.

"I'm looking for the tombstones that used to be here," she barked at Hammett, and he shuddered, never having heard a voice with such an icy edge. She sounded like she was spitting stones with every word. "I'm looking for my tombstones. Where are they?" she demanded angrily. "What did you do with them?" She raised her voice nearly to a shout.

"Her tone was accusatory. You could tell she had a personal interest in this," Hammett says. "She spoke with the despair of someone whose tombstones had been disturbed."

He glanced behind him to where his car was parked. The engine was still running. He wasn't sure how he would proceed. Was this a police matter? Perhaps he'd offer to drive her to the park office. When he turned back to where the woman had been standing, she was gone, vanished into thin air.

Hammett searched the grounds. After looking for about an hour he had found nothing. That night he told the story to his supervisor, Jerry Sword.

"Jerry walks over to his desk and picks up the very file he had been working on and hands it to me," Hammett recalls. "The title of the file was *Lost Cemetery: Point Lookout State Park, Picnic Area.*"

The men put two and two together and came up with a mystery that scared them both.

Sword related to Hammett what he had discovered in the records. A century ago, a lighthouse keeper noted in his log that several tombstones on the property were becoming endangered. The shore was eroding, and so were the graves. The five stones in the Taylor family plot were running out of time, wrote the keeper, and he feared they were about to wash into the bay. Four of the Taylor children had been buried in the plot here by their mother. She rested beside them in a fifth grave.

Hammett never laid eyes on the woman again.

Like Laura Berg, who must deal with memories of her phantom soldier, fleeting shadows, and unexplained sounds, Donnie Hammett lives with a disturbing memory. He, too, saw something that *wasn't there.*

When I tell people about Point Lookout, they often ask if I experienced any strange encounters with the unexplained during the filming. Did I see something that wasn't there, like Berg and Hammett? Or did I hear odd voices or unexplained sounds? And the answer is yes. There was a moment that gave me pause.

One gray, blustery February afternoon, months before we started production of *Haunted Lighthouses,* I met Don Hammett at Point

Lookout. Every location is scouted before it's formally included in the production schedule, and I elected to visit this site myself. Southern Maryland is only a few hours' drive from my home, and I never pass up an opportunity to see the Chesapeake. I brought along a small digital camera to take visual notes. I videotaped my interview with Don Hammett, and from basement to beacon I shot a fast overview of the lighthouse.

At some point late in the day, Hammett and I were standing on the back porch of one side of the lighthouse—the west side that faces the water. Hammett told me the story of former park manager Gerry Sword's pet German Shepherd. He was a very special animal. "He used to see people traveling on the old Civil War Road," said Hammett. "Sometimes he would sit for hours and watch traffic on that road. Of course there was no one ever really there, nobody travels that road anymore—not since the Civil War."

According to Hammett, the dog practically lived on the back porch where we stood talking. The winter sky grew dark as the sun dipped into the Potomac. I bid Hammett farewell, assuring him that I would let him know when we would be back to begin filming the Point Lookout segment of *Haunted Lighthouses*.

A few days later, when it was time to gather my Point Lookout video tape and notes and prepare my report, I was in for a surprise. The audio portion of the tape containing Hammett's story about the German Shepherd was odd, but at first I couldn't put my finger on it. Rewinding and repeating it, I heard a noise that shouldn't have been there. But it clearly was there. Startled, I scanned back to watch it a third time. It sounded like a dog barking. I was positive there hadn't been a dog anywhere near us that afternoon. A phone call to Don Hammett confirmed it—no dog. As we were about to sign off, he said something strange. "No, I can't explain that sound, but I'm not surprised by it, either."

So, that's my story—a barking dog that wasn't really there. Not much of a ghost story, but somehow I feel more connected to Point Lookout—to one of the spirits that seems to linger there—even if it was a dog.

From what historian Michael Humphries told me, I think he and the rest of them are just resigned to living in a world teeming with mysteries. Point Lookout is just one more mystery in a universe full of them. "Yeah, there's something going on here," Humphries sighed. "There's been too much: the photographs, the strange feelings, the voices. There's something going on here." But no one can explain what it is.

I said goodbye to the collection of spooks and phantoms at Point Lookout, setting out on the road for home. I'd like to say I kept moving and never looked back, but I did look back, just once and only for an instant. I turned around to behold this disturbing place for the last time—this dwelling that's perhaps not as empty as my crew and I once thought.

Is it a decrepit lighthouse and nothing more? Then what is that movement in the window, the fluttering wing of a black bird, or a shadow passing the glass? And what is that sound? A shutter banging in the wind, or a barking dog? I'm glad to surrender what remains behind to the coming darkness. I believe that whatever dwells here prefers it that way—to be left alone to its own ghostly devices.

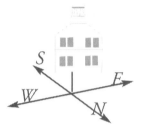

Travel Tips
Point Lookout Lighthouse

The U.S. Navy currently owns Point Lookout Lighthouse. And it's not a pretty sight. The chainlink fence, presumably erected to keep out small animals and curious tourists, doesn't do much for the nineteenth-century feel of the lighthouse. The side yard is a nasty jumble of satellite dishes. High-tech communications gear is in our national interest, but it doesn't do much for the neighborhood.

And the lighthouse itself is a real fixer-upper. But if the Maryland State Parks Department has its way, Point Lookout Lighthouse will belong to Maryland someday, so this historic property can be restored properly and opened for public tours. Until then, you'll just have to settle for stolen peaks through links of wire fence. After sunset, it's not the lighthouse that lights up, it's the backyard. An automated beacon sits on top of a skeleton tower behind the house.

Point Lookout is a well-kept secret at the southern tip of Maryland's western peninsula. The state's trendy Eastern Shore grabs all the attention with its crab derbies and sailboat shows. But over here, on the unfashionable west side, this bucolic shore is ignored, although the woods and waterscapes are gorgeous. You might be tempted to call it land's end, or road's end. That's how you'll know you're here.

From Annapolis, take Route 2 south, which will become Route 4. After a stretch of two-lane blacktop, the route becomes a highway. Cross the Patuxent River at the Solomons. The Calvert Marine Museum is worth a stop to take in some Chesapeake Bay history.

Returning to Route 4, at the intersection of Route 4 and Route 235, head south for about 15 minutes. Pick up Route 5 and pass through the little town of Scotland. Signs direct you to Point Lookout State Park.

If you stay on Route 4 for a few more miles and then backtrack to pick up Route 5, you can enjoy a ghostly detour to Leonardtown, Maryland, and discover the haunting spirit of Moll Dyer. Moll was a strange hermit who lived in the area in the late 1700s. Her wild, eccentric behavior got her into trouble with the townsfolk. They came to suspect Moll was a witch. One frigid winter, they drove her from the ramshackle, one-room hut she called home. She fled to the river. Days later Moll's body was discovered—frozen in a kneeling position on a huge boulder by the water.

When they removed Moll Dyer's body, they found the impression of her hand and knee etched in the stone. And to exact revenge for her misery, Moll's ghost began tormenting the locals. To this day they see her eerie specter floating over the woods where she lived. Over time, countless people have claimed to fall victim to dark feelings when they visit here. Others have supposedly experienced agonizing pains. Some people claim Moll Dyer's spirit is still active today. Ask about her at the St. Mary's Historical Society in Leonardtown, where you'll see the stone that bears Moll's knee and hand prints (410-475-2467).

Returning to the road to Point Lookout State Park, signs will direct you past Scotland, Maryland, and into the park. Traverse the park road to the office and museum. It's not necessary to stop here, but it's worthwhile. Inside a little museum, where imagination more than capital funding is apparent, are highly original displays pertinent to Point Lookout's history, all done on a shoestring budget.

Past the museum are a picnic area, fishing pier, swimming beach, and another recommended stop, the Point Lookout Confederate Cemetery. Interestingly, two very different monuments have been erected here, one state, the other federal. A list of the names of known dead is included. Many of the three thousand or so who perished here are not among them. Their remains were never found.

The park road ends at a breakwater. Look to your right and you'll see the lighthouse about a quarter of a mile away.

The good news? The original Point Lookout Lighthouse has

somehow survived intact—or at least its shell is still standing. But bad news—no daily public access or regular lighthouse tours.

For more information, park hours, and schedule of special events, call the Point Lookout State Park office. The staff is very helpful. But plan to be out of the area before dark. The park closes at sundown and the lighthouse comes alive, so to speak, with strange visitors from the past. I suspect you wouldn't find them very desirable companions.

Point Lookout Lighthouse
Point Lookout State Park
301-872-5688

—∞—

As you drive north on the peninsula, consider a stop at the Lighthouse Inn in Solomons, Maryland, for lunch or dinner. This two-story restaurant/hangout is a popular place for thirsty locals and hungry boaters. The seafood is fresh, most notably the crab cakes. The bar is fun and usually buzzing, and it was built as a replica of a skipjack boat. Try to steer your host or hostess toward a window table so you can enjoy the sailboat traffic in busy Solomons Harbor.

Lighthouse Inn
Solomons, Maryland
410-326-2444

—ᴍ—

An antique-filled bed and breakfast called the Victorian Inn in Solomons was recommended to us, but too late to check in during this visit. By that time we were already settled at the Solomons Holiday Inn, near the restaurant mentioned above. As chain hotels go, this was a good one with fine marina views and hearty breakfasts featuring, no surprise, a crab omelet.

Solomons Holiday Inn
410-326-6311

—ᴍ—

If there is a next time, and enough rooms for the crew and gear, I'll consider the Victorian Inn with its charming harbor location and homey decor.

Victorian Inn
410-326-4811

Ernie the Ghost
New London Ledge Lighthouse

Connecticut

In the harbor of New London, Connecticut, all is not what it seems. Why is an elegant three-story mansion floating out on the water? Is this grand, Victorian house some sort of castaway? Oddly, it's a lighthouse, nestled on a stone ledge, surrounded by the sea, and—strangest of all— inhabited by the spirit of a forsaken keeper.

ounded in 1646, the city of New London, Connecticut, began as a bustling seagoing village, and it's been a busy port ever since. The whaling industry started right here in 1874, thriving for more than a hundred years. At its peak, at least seventy-five whaling vessels were based in New London. Today, the harbor is home to all varieties of marine craft—cutters, yachts, cruisers, submarines, as well as a fleet of ferryboats.

From New London, the Thames River flows into Long Island Sound. Most Americans—and undoubtedly all Londoners—would be surprised to hear the locals pronounce *Thames*. Strangely, in New England the "h" is not silent, and Thames rhymes with James. But no matter how you say it, this busy waterway has always been considered one of the finest deep-water ports on the Atlantic coast.

Now look closely—another peculiarity about this harbor will strike you. It's the lighthouse—Ledge Light, as it's called. Some people say it looks like an old brick Victorian house that fell out of the sky and landed smack in the center of a cement slab floating in the harbor. Nevertheless, this misplaced structure is a familiar site to countless skippers who pass it everyday. And for many, the rich legend attached to its past is their favorite ghost story.

"If you ask anyone about Ledge Light," author and lighthouse historian Elinor De Wire reflects, "they can't tell you what year it was built, they can't tell you the architectural style, they can't tell you any of the important details about its career. But they *can* tell you about Ernie—Ernie the ghost."

U.S. Coast Guard Photo

The unusual design of Ledge Light makes it look like it's floating in the harbor at New London, CT.

"You hear a thousand different stories about Ernie," adds New England historian and storyteller, Bill Thomson of Maine. "Everyone has their own slant on what he does."

"Ernie far outshines anything else we know about the lighthouse," Elinor remarks with eyebrows raised and a touch of irony in her voice.

For decades, the legend of Ernie has been passed down by skippers, light keepers, and Coast Guardsmen. On cold dark nights, wherever these crusty seamen gather, Ernie tales are spun. Normally stern types who aren't prone to dabble in the supernatural realm have a story or two to tell. This ghost can summon up mystical curiosity in the most unlikely soul.

No one is quite sure who he really was, how he fits into the long history of Ledge Light, or even why he's called Ernie. But there is plenty of speculation.

Brae Rafferty is the director of Project Oceanography, fondly called Project "O," and he heads up the New London Ledge Light Foundation as well. These two groups are responsible for lighthouse care and operation. Brae speculates that the man we now call Ernie—whatever his real name was—must have lived at the lighthouse sometime in the mid-1920s, long before the U.S. Coast Guard took charge of all American lighthouses.

"There was a period of time when record keeping wasn't the best and log books were neglected," he says, explaining why we may never know for certain whether there actually was a flesh and blood Ernie.

Inadequate records were one problem; another was rapid turnover. "During this period of lighthouse history," explains Brae, "you almost had to go down to the local bar to find someone to come out here and man the light. It got to be very lonely in this place and most people were just not cut out for it."

The name Ernie may have been dreamed up long ago by some imaginative Coast Guardsman anxious to give the ghost a convenient handle. As far as Brae Rafferty can tell, the archives include no Ernies who resided at Ledge Light. But there is an intriguing story floating around out there, sketchy as the details might be.

It happened that a keeper named John Randolf served briefly at Ledge Light, sometime in the 1920s. Who knows, he might have been one of those unsuspecting souls cajoled out of a local pub—or speakeasy, since this was the Prohibition era—and conned into the job of lightkeeper.

Could Randolf be the legendary Ernie? Nobody knows for sure. But it is said that when Randolf first arrived at this mansion on the Ledge, at his side was his new wife, a pretty young woman barely out of her teens. Except for her youth and beauty, however, we know nothing about her, not even her name.

According to the most popular version of the legend, Randolf was twice her age, twice unlucky at love, and doubly determined to make this marriage last. New London's rumor mill had him pegged as a gambler, a loser, in fact, who squandered a small fortune. Apparently his first wife went out the door with the fortune.

As the story unfolds, Randolf finally reformed, and he began his search for stability. Strangely, to Randolf that meant finding a teenage bride. And if settling down was his goal, he had surely come to the worst possible place—a lonely lighthouse surrounded by water. Perhaps it was just romance on Randolf's mind. And make no mistake, for the first few months, romance was certainly in the air at Ledge Light. The couple couldn't keep their eyes, or hands, off one another.

Given enough time, though, the honeymoon ended. Just months into their marriage, Randolf's wife was threatening to leave him. Overnight the young woman seemed to lose patience with life on this isolated block of damp cement. People say that the couple argued bitterly, that he begged her to stay, but she coldly shrugged off his appeals. She called him pathetic.

"This lighthouse is our home and it will kill me if you leave," cried Randolf. His desperate pleas made her even more determined to escape.

It was just a matter of time. For the impetuous young bride, this floating mansion was more of a prison than home. Day after day she watched ships pass and saw life, too, passing her by.

One evening a ship stopped—a ferryboat on its way to New York—and the young wife ran off with the captain.

When the keeper discovered her betrayal, he was devastated. Standing on the concrete pier, looking up at the beacon, his thoughts were dark. He slowly climbed to the highest level of the lighthouse, up to the lantern room sixty-five feet above the sea. He shoved open the heavy steel door leading to the roof and stepped out into the salty air. His gaze riveted on the misty blue horizon, and he watched the departing ships, wondering which vessel held his runaway bride. He stood stock-still, as though he might never move from the spot again.

Suddenly, he did move, pulling out a sharp blade, cutting his own throat, and leaping to his death. His beautiful young wife had become the jilted keeper's downfall.

The next day Randolf's body was found draped over the edge of the concrete pier, his arm dangling limply in the water, his black light keeper's hat bobbing on the harbor's gray surface, his blood splattered on the chalky cement.

The Lighthouse Board wasted no time in appointing a new keeper, selecting a mild-mannered, pipe-smoking gentleman. He was accompanied by his loyal dog, an aging Irish Setter, anxious to remain the keeper's faithful companion during his duty at this isolated light station.

For a time, all seemed normal out on Ledge Light. But before long, strange things began to happen inside the lighthouse—bizarre occurrences, at first unexplained, but then suspected of being the work of an active spirit.

The steel door to the roof mysteriously opened and closed on its own. Footsteps went clanging up to the lantern room when no one could be seen in the stairway. Lights were turned on and off unexpectedly.

"Ernie is perhaps the most colorful lighthouse ghost you'd ever want to meet," declares Elinor De Wire. Colorful is one word for him, but according to some people, annoying is more accurate.

"Ernie is what you'd consider a playful ghost," Elinor says. "He does tricky little things. He steals tools, he drinks coffee that's left out in cups, rearranges the books on the library shelf."

Historian Bill Thomson adds that Ernie's presence has been experienced by keepers and their guests for generations. "Ernie turns on the foghorn," says Thomson, "and sometimes he'll polish the brass or clean the windows."

"Nobody can explain what they're seeing," he adds. "Regular people like you and me are witnesses to unbelievable things. There's something strange going on here, that's for sure."

"Ghosts are notorious pranksters," notes Mark Nesbitt, author of *The Ghosts of Gettysburg*, who is familiar with the legend of Ernie. "Ghosts actually seem to have a sense of humor. Ernie's behavior sure fits that description."

Ernie's shenanigans leave us pondering an even greater mystery. For some unfathomable reason—perhaps one that can be grasped only by a ghost—this so-called light-hearted trickster seems to be the spirit of a forlorn lighthouse keeper whose wife abandoned him and whose life ended in tragedy. Wouldn't you expect this ghost to have a darker personality?

"That's right," quips Bill Thomson. "If ghosts were predictable, you'd expect Ernie to be angry and sinister and full of revenge. He's not. Why? It's anybody's guess. But don't forget, it doesn't have to make sense. He's a ghost!"

Not that Ernie doesn't occasionally show a slightly darker side.

"A U.S. Coast Guardsman I spoke to said he was in bed one night trying to go to sleep," Elinor De Wire reports. "Suddenly his pillow was lifted up beside him, put over his face, and he was fighting with some invisible nemesis for several minutes, only to find later there was nobody in the room. He had this sense that Ernie was in there with him."

Normally—if that's a word that can be applied here—Ernie is invisible. But whenever he *is* seen, it's in shadows. And curiously, only women have ever laid eyes on him. That's a part of the legend Elinor De Wire finds especially strange.

"The story is that a woman might glimpse him in a mirror," she says, "or spot him out the corner of her eye. But men aren't able to catch sight of him."

Once in the 1940s, a keeper's wife claimed she had encountered Ernie. She woke up in the middle of the night and caught someone standing at the foot of her bed. It was a tall, bearded fellow dressed in a rain slicker. In her recollection, he resembled a sea captain. She reported that both his scruffy white beard and glossy yellow slicker were dripping wet, as though he had just trudged in from the sea.

The poor woman let out a whale of a scream and the haunting figure vanished in thin air. The only thing that remained was a puddle of water where he had been standing.

"The morning after this incident is supposed to have occurred," Bill Thomson tells us, "the lady packed up all her belongings and moved out. I don't know whether the keeper went with her or not, but she was really scared. She might have heard Ernie was a friendly ghost, but she wasn't taking any chances."

Over the years, letters to friends and scribbles in lighthouse logs began to tell the story of a restless spirit meddling in the most mundane ways with the lives of busy keepers. A lighthouse keeper identified only as David told psychic investigators that he and his colleague at Ledge Light heard doors slam mysteriously and someone walking on the third floor when no one was up there. They also heard a refrigerator door open and close on its own, repeatedly, all night. Furniture was moved about, especially appliances like radios and TV sets. Of course, being men, they never had a glimpse of Ernie, the suspected perpetrator. But they certainly believed he was in the lighthouse somewhere.

A New England psychic who investigated the reports of paranormal activity at New London Ledge Light once said, "He just wants attention. Sadly, this ghost is trying desperately to make itself known."

Brae Rafferty, arguably the foremost expert on legends and lore surrounding New London Ledge Lighthouse, admits he's never seen or heard Ernie himself. But he knows people who have tangled with the ghost.

"One time, a couple of fishermen stopped by to visit the keeper," Brae explains. "They tied up their boat beside the lighthouse, and joined the keeper for dinner."

Brae tells us that during the meal, the keeper brought up the subject of Ernie the ghost, a spirit he believed had been hanging around Ledge Light for many years.

At the mere mention of a ghost, both fishermen shook their heads and laughed in delight. They weren't buying that tall tale, scoffed one of the men.

"When it came time to leave the lighthouse, their boat was nowhere to be seen," Brae continues. "No one else was around. These two were experienced guys who certainly knew how to tie off their boat. Yet there it was, cast off. Coincidence? I don't know. But they sure became believers on the spot."

Brae recalls hearing another story related to the origin of Ernie, an incident that dates back some years before the lighthouse was even built. "Very few people know about this one," he confides.

Several years ago, Brae met a woman whose grandfather had helped build the lighthouse nearly a century earlier. During the meeting, Brae asked her about Ernie. "She had never heard of him," Brae says, "but she told me her grandfather used to spin another equally strange yarn."

During construction of the lighthouse, so the story goes, odd things happened repeatedly. Tools fell off the scaffolding without explanation. Other items disappeared mysteriously from the site. Parts of the new structure suffered unexplained damage and had to be repaired or rebuilt. The woman told Brae about her grandfather's frequent mentions of eerie sounds around the lighthouse and strange shadows he saw at night.

Brae decided to probe a little deeper into the story, so he headed for the library. What his research uncovered adds up to an intriguing tale of tragedy. And it casts some doubt on the theory that Ernie is the spirit of lovelorn Keeper Randolf.

Brae points, calling our attention to a dark patch of water about eighty or so yards from the lighthouse. He gestures to the horizon where a distant rock pile is visible just above the water line. The rocks appear sharp and malevolent. Brae informs us the spot is called Black Ledge, an apt name for such an evil looking stretch of water. Many ships have become unsuspecting victims of Black Ledge.

Just before the turn of the twentieth century, about a decade before the lighthouse went up, Black Ledge was the scene of a deadly ship wreck, one of many over the years, but this one especially tragic. Among the dozen or so people on board the doomed vessel was a newly married couple from New London.

Most passengers perished, but the husband was able to swim ashore while his wife was nowhere to be found. For several days the distraught man combed the beach in search of a clue, desperately seeking any trace of his wife. But he never found her body.

One evening, while pacing the deserted beach, the heartsick husband made an abrupt turn into the surf, out toward the killer rocks of Black Ledge. Witnesses said he wore a smile, like a person feeling relief after making a big decision. His walk was steady, his gaze fixed, as though he was on his way to meet someone he knew awaited him. The strong waves kept pushing him back to shore, but he struggled through the icy water up to his chest, and soon it was over his head. The young man swallowed the sea. He chose to end his own life rather than live another day without his bride.

We looked out to Black Ledge where the couple had perished. On this grim note, we sat for a moment in silence.

"So . . . perhaps there was already a spirit here." Brae smiles broadly at this intriguing prospect. "From the very day they topped off the lighthouse, maybe it had a resident ghost."

Is it possible that more than one spirit haunts this lighthouse? Is Ernie really a lot of Ernies—an entire legion of ghosts?

Whoever he, she, or they are, we asked Brae if the spirit called Ernie has any legitimate importance to the history of Ledge Light.

He laughs and nods his head affirmatively. "Ernie is key to this lighthouse. All lighthouses have something unique about them. This one is a unique structure on the outside, sure, but it also has a very lively ghost. And he's very much a part of its past."

Today, the doors of the lighthouse are bolted, the windows locked, and the beacon is automated. No one stays on New London Ledge. At least, no one who's alive.

Postscript

Help sometimes comes out of nowhere, and in strange ways. On this cold slab of concrete, strange seems to be a pretty normal thing.

One encounter I had here still haunts me. It was late on our final afternoon of filming at the lighthouse. The sun was dipping into the harbor and a special time of day for filmmakers was beginning. The harbor wore a sash of sunlight across its middle, the orange sunbeams dancing on the wakes of small boats.

Our ride back to shore wasn't due for at least another hour. One more shot and we were out of there. But first we had to set up the scene, and we were stumped. Sitting on the edge of the cement pier, I wondered how we were going to capture several takes of a lighthouse keeper's hat floating in the water—without the hat floating away.

One member of the crew was in the lighthouse looking for a long stick with which to snag the hat and pull it back. He returned empty-handed. I called his attention to a small speck on the horizon. The speck was moving toward us and I was sure it hadn't been there a moment earlier. Closer and closer it came—now it was making noise. Speechless, we stared—forgetting all about the hat dilemma.

In a few moments, we knew company was coming. The speck had turned into a lone kayaker, one who was paddling like crazy, and shouting, "Hey there! What are you doing out here?" It was at once strange and comical. There's no land in sight and no other living creatures except the seabirds screeching over our heads, and here comes this guy in a five-foot kayak acting like the lighthouse inspector.

Turned out he thought our explanation for what we were doing was pretty odd too—if he even believed us at all. But he did help with the hat, retrieving it between takes—four times, as a matter of fact. He waved goodbye and paddled off.

I can still see that guy disappearing into the big orange ball of sinking sun. *Who was he anyway?* I wondered.

A couple of hours later, back at the dock, when it turned out none of the locals had ever seen this kayaker, one of them volunteered a theory. In one of his many guises, it was Ernie—Ernie the ghost.

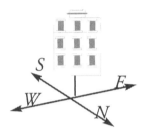

Travel Tips
New London Ledge Lighthouse

Erected in 1909, Ledge Light is still active. It marks the dangerous ledge of rock that surrounds it—the dreaded Black Ledge. The tower and fourth order Fresnel lens rise out of the center of the roof of a three-story brick structure situated on a concrete pier.

They say the architecture is unusual but not unique. Truthfully, though, I've never seen another one like it.

In 1987, the U.S. Coast Guard automated the beacon.

At the time of our location filming, public access to New London Ledge Lighthouse was limited to private tours, special events, and Project Oceanology cruises launched from Avery Point. The annual Halloween tour conducted by the New London Ledge Light Foundation is popular. Other tour events are featured throughout the year as well, according to Brae Rafferty, director of Project Oceanology, or Project "O" as they call it. An approximately two-and-a-half-hour educational cruise conducted by Project "O" includes a visit to the lighthouse. It departs from Avery Point's University of Connecticut campus during the summer season only. There is a fee for the cruise and you can call for updated information. Viewed from the mainland, the lighthouse is an indistinct little spot on the horizon. You'll have to find transportation to get out there.

Small sightseeing boats are for hire at the dock. While some are available for tours by the hour, others charge a flat rate. During our location filming for *Haunted Lighthouses*, we kicked into our haggling mode. Try it—it's a buyer's market off season. When the script called for a wide exterior shot of the lighthouse, we ambled down to the dock and made an offer. We found great deals on short hops into the harbor, and shot some terrific film of the lighthouse at sunset that way.

You can hop on a ferry, but no haggling. Three lines are represented here: Block Island, Long Island, and Rhode Island. They all pass the lighthouse on the way in and out of the harbor. A ferry leaves from Ferry Street for Block Island, Rhode Island. For ferry information, call 860-442-7891.

New London Ledge Lighthouse
Project Oceanology at Avery Point
800-364-8472, 860-445-9007

—⁓—

For lunch we enjoyed Timothy's on Bank Street, in downtown New London. The cuisine leans toward Italian. For example, seasoned olive oil is served for fresh bread dipping, and lots of pasta is available. But the proprietors would like you to think of it as a contemporary bistro. It's a real find in New London, which seems to operate in the shadow of grander tourist spots like Mystic.

Our tight schedule permitted one lunch stop only at Timothy's. But dinners looked tempting. The several specialties included flounder coated in crushed pecans and lean duckling with a berry demi-glace. Crab and lobster bisque with a splash of sherry is a locally well-known specialty of the house. It made a terrific lunch.

Timothy's
181 Bank Street
New London, CT
860-437-0526

On Noank Harbor, there's a well-known landmark hugging the shore. No, not another haunted lighthouse—and the scariest thing you're going to see there is a two-pound live lobster writhing about. Abbott's Lobster in the Rough is a bare-bones lobster shack with picnic tables inside and out, offering a lobster feast practically as good as any in New England, including Maine. Head south on SR 215 from Mystic and watch for signs to Noank.

Abbott's Lobster in the Rough

117 Pearl St.

Noank, CT

(860) 536-7719

One evening I decided to treat the crew to a good meal at a wonderful restaurant, a place I'd been returning to for years—a cozy inn in Stonington, Connecticut, only about twenty minutes or so from New London. On the drive I raved about the rustic, nautical ambience and chatted up the food. Great grilled mussels in garlic wine sauce, fresh-caught seafood, twice-baked potatoes would all be fabulous. Everyone was starved.

We parked the van and my heart sunk—the kind of feeling you get when you misplace something, like your wallet. Only this was a misplaced restaurant. I knew exactly where it had been, but now it was a flat, empty lot between two buildings. The crew looked at me blankly. This was embarrassing.

And then, I was saved by a dog walker. A fire had destroyed the place, burning it right down to the ground. It had happened only a few weeks earlier.

We enjoyed good dinners in a fine restaurant up the street, one that could have been a real winner under other circumstances. But I was uneasy all evening. Memories can be as haunting as ghosts.

(Good news—I understand the Harbor View has been resurrected and opened on its former site.)

Harbor View

Bank Street,

Stonington, Connecticut

—m—

For upscale lodging in the New London-Mystic area, check out the Inn at Mystic, a turn-of-the-century hotel in an elegant mansion on thirteen acres overlooking Long Island Sound. Among the many famous guests in the history of the Inn at Mystic is a honeymoon couple familiar to film buffs: Bogey and Bacall. (If anybody at the inn knows, they're not giving out the couple's room number.) The inn is top rate and off peak season it can be surprisingly affordable.

With a view of the sea, the elegant restaurant, called Flood Tide, is first class and priced accordingly. You might save it for an anniversary, or then again, just go ahead and splurge. Something from the menu to help you decide—"Native Lobster in risotto with fresh asparagus finished in sun-dried tomato oil." Or—"Pan-seared colossal sea scallops with orange basil compote."

Inn at Mystic is only a short drive from New London, two miles south of I-95 Exit 90.

Inn at Mystic

US 1 & CT 27

Mystic, CT

800-237-2415

—∞—

You shouldn't visit Mystic without a stop at Mystic Seaport. Some people say it's our country's leading maritime museum. It promotes an understanding of life in a seaport in the mid-nineteenth century through its vast exhibits, historic houses, shops, and trade buildings. Special events take place throughout the year. And, of course, they have lots of things to sell you, as well.

Mystic Seaport
75 Greenmanville Ave.
Mystic, CT
Daily 9 A.M. to 6 P.M. (seasonal)
Admission charge
1-888-9SEAPORT

Haunted Harbor
Boston Light

Massachusetts

Boston Lighthouse and the surrounding harbor islands are steeped in American history. Yet some people say it's more mystery than history you sense as you wend your way through Boston Harbor, then stop to climb the aging beacon. And when something creeps up your spine, you may wonder—is America's oldest lighthouse also its most haunted?

S hips have been passing a lighthouse on Little Brewster Island since 1716, longer than any lighthouse site in America. Today, Boston Light stands tall like a sentinel posted at the entrance to Boston Harbor, a body of water that is arguably America's most historic—and, perhaps, most haunted. Over the past four centuries, dozens of islands that dot Boston Harbor have seen plundering pirates run aground, major battles won and lost, prisoners confined, and thousands felled by war and disease. The aftermath may have left the surrounding waters brimming with restless spirits.

The harbor islands are as ancient as they are magnificent. When the glaciers of the last Ice Age receded, about fifteen thousand years ago, they left behind mounds of rock, gravel, and soil. When the ocean waters rose, the islands of Boston Harbor were born.

Holly Richardson, an officer of the Metropolitan District Commission (MDC), one of the agencies that oversees the islands, serves as a tour interpreter for thousands of visitors to Boston Harbor. Holly's love for the harbor islands goes far beyond her job.

To film the islands and lighthouse for *Haunted Lighthouses*, we are traveling with a group that includes Holly Richardson and John Forbes, president of Friends of Boston Harbor.

"You're so close yet so far away," says Holly, noting that from the shores of most of the islands you can see the Boston skyline. "Yet you feel so isolated because you're on an island. It just makes you feel like you're in another time."

"I think people do feel a presence of spirits out there. It's a mag-

*Boston Harbor Light, the nation's oldest lighthouse, believed to be haunted by
spirits right out of the pages of American history.*

ical feeling. It's a place for one's imagination to wander." Holly flashes a smile, leaving us to wonder what mysteries she imagines hang
over the islands.

Over the millennia, these islands have had many inhabitants.
Archeological remains found on Peddock's Island, the Harbor's
largest land mass, suggest that more than six thousand years ago,
Peddock's was home to Native Americans.

More recently, but still nearly two centuries ago, one of the
greatest imaginations of all time went wandering in Boston Harbor.
Edgar Allan Poe spent time here, and believe it or not, he was born
in Boston, in 1809—a big surprise to many folks in Baltimore where

Poe died but spent very little of his life. But that's another story.

In 1827, under the name Edwin A. Perry, Poe enlisted in the U.S. Army, First Massachusetts Heavy Artillery, and was stationed at Fort Independence on Castle Island—which was still an island at that time. Some people believe that the master of the macabre was inspired to write his famous short story, *The Cask of Amontillado*, after hearing about an incident at Fort Independence.

Poe was told that a decade earlier, a popular soldier, Lt. Robert F. Massie, was killed in a duel by the fort's dreaded bully, Lt. Gustavus Drane. That duel supposedly took place on Christmas Day, 1817, and Massie's fellow soldiers were outraged at the result. A group of them tricked Drane into becoming drunk and led him to the dungeon. There they chained him down and sealed up the vault. Drane was left to die a slow, horrible death in this makeshift tomb.

In Poe's story, a cad by the name of Fortunato, a greedy wine connoisseur, is led into the catacombs of the narrator's cellar under the pretense of tasting a rare Italian wine, Amontillado. Searching the catacombs and vaults—"insufferably damp" Poe calls them— Fortunato is tricked into becoming drunk. The narrator shackles him to the granite wall with chains and begins to seal him in a recessed niche with bricks and mortar. Poe's narrator offers this cold-blooded account of laying bricks to imprison Fortunato in the tomb:

> I had scarcely laid the first tier of the masonry

when I discovered that the intoxication of Fortunato had in great measure worn off. The earliest indication I had of this was a low moaning cry from the depth of the recess. It was not the cry of a drunken man. There was then a long and obstinate silence. I laid the second tier, and the third, and the fourth; and then I heard the furious vibrations of the chain.

Despite hearing the chains and further cries from behind the wall, the narrator finishes his job and leaves Fortunato to suffer an awful death. Poe's dark tale is strikingly similar to the story of Captain Drane. Whether Poe actually based his story on the Drane incident has never been officially confirmed. And I must warn you, many feel the story is apocryphal. But there are those who feel the coincidences are too great for a connection not to exist.

Poe's story ends with this hideous entombment. The story of Captain Drane continues on from there. Immediately following Drane's agonizing demise, soldiers reported an unearthly specter floating over the fort wearing an officer's uniform. It scared the soldiers half to death, and some of them actually deserted. Sightings of this bizarre apparition have supposedly persisted to the present.

Yet another rumor has made the rounds of Boston Harbor, tempting some people to draw more unsettling conclusions. A group of workmen were digging under Fort Independence. When their shovels clunked into an underground brick wall and they broke through it, the workmen were shocked to find a human skeleton. The most amazing discovery of all was the skeleton's attire. Clinging to the man's bare bones was an 1812 officer's uniform. Is this story true? You may want to explore the matter further, but there seems to be enough evidence to fuel speculation.

Another gem in the necklace of harbor islands is Gallop. Situated near Little Brewster and the Boston Light, Gallop Island was once occupied by the French, later used as barracks in the Civil War, and then turned into a site for a smallpox hospital in the late nineteenth century. Paranormal experts have put forth a theory that links suffering and death to spiritual unrest. Some say Gallop Island has had its share of both, and further suspect that an eerie presence lingers here.

As our boat and our imaginations wander past Gallop Island, we stay our course to Little Brewster. Glancing starboard we spot a small clump of land in the water—all that remains of the mysterious vanishing island known as Nix's Mate. This is a story locals love to tell. Where did the island go, and why?

This island was cursed about three centuries ago—at least that's what they say—by the unlucky mate of Captain Nix. According to the legend, a shipmate was charged with killing his captain. He vehemently denied the crime. But his hotheaded shipmates weren't buying it, and they took him to the nearest island where they prepared to hang him. As the damp rope was slipped over his head, before he swung from the makeshift gallows of stones and driftwood, he screamed wildly at his accusers, cursing the island forever. "I swear I am not guilty," he cried. "If you hang me, I promise this island will wash away, disappearing into the sea. My innocence will be proved."

The island of Nix's Mate was an ample twelve acres in those days. Today, at high tide, it's barely visible. It did shrink, no question about that. And boaters who pass too close to this little nub of land sometimes hear the ghastly laugh of Nix's Mate himself, taunting them, rubbing in the fact that his curse proved him right. When the island finally disappears altogether, the mystery will always remain.

Farther out toward the lighthouse, we encounter the most mysterious of all the islands of Boston Harbor. George's Island is home to a spine-tingling tale of love, death, and intrigue—not to mention a resident ghost.

The story begins when the Civil War was raging, and a young Confederate officer from South Carolina named Lanier was captured and imprisoned at Fort Warren on George's Island. Fort Warren is a massive granite structure that appears to be nearly impenetrable, but not to a determined woman who was driven by her love for her husband and her hatred of the enemy.

After his capture, Lanier managed to get a message to his wife, Melanie, at their home outside Charleston. A brave, resourceful woman, Melanie Lanier concocted a plan to travel to Boston and rescue her husband. After weeks of hardship on the road, she finally reached Boston Harbor. There she fell in with some Confederate sympathizers who outfitted her with men's clothing, a gun, and a boat. She rowed to the island, miraculously penetrated the fort's security, and entered the Corridor of Dungeons where her husband was incarcerated.

With the help of the sympathizers, she located his cell. Weeping tears of joy, Melanie ran to her husband. While they embraced, a guard heard the sounds of their passionate reunion. Warily, he approached the cell. Melanie had come this far; she was not going to permit a lone sentry to ruin her plan. She pulled out her gun, aimed it at the Yankee, and fired.

Smoke filled the small cell and Melanie's eyes burned. She turned to the man who stood over the dead body and started to reach for his hand. Then she saw it was the guard. Her gun had misfired. The shot went wild and killed her husband.

Melanie Lanier was rushed by a band of shouting sentries, knocked to the ground, and dragged to the fort's darkest dungeon. Worse than a spy, she was a murderer. At a hastily arranged trial, she was sentenced to hang. The only kindness shown to Melanie was the permission she was granted to wear woman's clothing to her execution. But a long black cape was the only female attire they could find in the fort. When she dropped through the trap door and met eternity dangling at the end of a rope, that's what Melanie Lanier was wearing.

Dolly Snow, whose father Edgar Rowe Snow wrote many

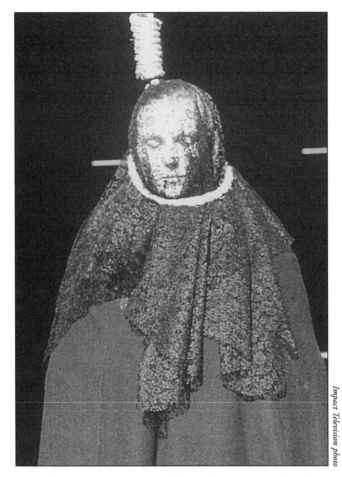

Impact Television photo

One of the creepiest ghosts of Boston Harbor is known as the "Lady in Black."

famous stories about Boston Harbor, including one about Melanie Lanier, explains that over the years many of the fort's staff and visitors claim to have seen the "Lady in Black." And you guessed it, when she's sighted, it's always a long black cape she's wearing. A terrorizing sight it must be, too. Startled sentries have even fired upon the apparition.

"One night shortly after Melanie's death, a sentry felt invisible hands gripping his neck," says Dolly. "He fell to the ground, then looked up and saw that choking him was none other than Melanie Lanier, the lady who had been hanged seven weeks before."

The best time to see the Lady in Black is right after sunset, believed to be the hour she was hanged. "There have been many more sightings," Dolly says. "In the last century there have been at least twenty-eight sightings officially recorded."

She seems to float rather than walk, although one account did mention her "creeping through the night." Her black cape touches the ground, a black veil covers her head and drapes around her shoulders. No one has seen her face, if she even has a face.

In a hushed voice, a tour guide told me about his experience with the Lady in Black. "She drifted along the ramparts as though a

A ghost known as the "Lady in Black" has been seen many times by staff and visitors creeping along the ramparts of Fort Warren on Georges Island.

stiff breeze was pushing her forward. But there was no breeze that night. She never even glanced my way. She didn't make a sound. I felt like I was witnessing something that wasn't a part of this world—maybe something I really wasn't supposed to see. But I did see it, and I'll never forget it."

"She's often seen in the Corridor of Dungeons," adds Dolly Snow, "where she was briefly reunited with her husband before she shot him. People see her peering out of the musketry opening—perhaps still looking for him, or looking for her freedom."

Nothing in the records, official or unofficial, indicates that the ghost of Melanie Lanier ever drifted over to Little Brewster Island where Boston Light presides, although the nearby beacon burned brightly on that night in 1861, when Melanie was hanged as a spy and murderess. The light was in service then, just as it is today, flashing a powerful white beam every ten seconds, visible for twenty-seven miles out to sea.

The history of Boston Light closely parallels the history of our nation. A tower was built on Little Brewster Island in 1716. It was America's first lighthouse. Suffering damage during the Revolutionary War from both the American and British sides, it required extensive rebuilding in 1783. As a teenager, Ben Franklin wrote a "doggeral ditty" about the lighthouse and the drowning of its first keeper, George Worthylake, a tragedy that is said to have intrigued Franklin.

Today the lighthouse holds the distinction of remaining the last manned light station in the United States—the only lighthouse in America that's not automated.

"We thank Senator Ted Kennedy for that," says John Forbes, president of the Friends of Boston Harbor. "He passed the bill that requires Boston Light to have an actual person on site twenty-four hours a day. This is added expense for the government, but given the important history of this place, Boston Light deserves it."

"When you think about how old it is, how permanent—and how much history it's seen, this little island is an awe-inspiring place," Forbes explains. "Think about how many lives it's saved. Every time I see that lighthouse, it's close to a religious experience. That thing talks to me sometimes."

And according to some accounts, what it says can be a little frightening.

It was a cool, early spring afternoon when I arrived at Little Brewster Island with the camera crew. John Forbes, who knows this island and all of Boston Harbor like the back of his hand, served as a guide. The keeper on duty was Richard Himelrich, U. S. Coast Guard, who welcomed us heartily. He told us right up front to call him Rick.

Rick and I had talked by phone a week before our arrival, and he told me we were free to visit and bring all our TV equipment, but we probably wouldn't get see any ghosts. They don't like cameras. By telephone, three hundred or so miles away, I could tell he was wearing a broad smile.

The day had started out sunny, but heavy gray clouds moved in fast. The mood of the harbor turned gloomy too, and the color of the water darkened to ink. But a frisky dog can do wonders to cheer up a party. As our small craft approached Little Brewster, a large black Lab bounded down the weathered wooden dock. Her name was Sam. And talk about a smile—from ear to ear. Here was a dog who lived on an isolated island and loved to have company come calling.

Trailing behind Sam, Rick Himelrich came into view. Rick is a youthful man sporting a casual blue Coast Guard uniform and a glint in his eye that said he could stand a little company himself. He led us up a long, twisting paved walkway, past giant glacial stones washed smooth by eons in the sea. We plopped down on the stones to talk.

It happens that Rick does feel a presence here, not of ghosts exactly, but of the dozens of keepers who served before him—of history. He speaks of the former keepers as though they had all left a little part of themselves behind. "Imagine all the keepers who have come and gone out here. I think a lot about them," he says with reverence.

"You climb those seventy-six steps and you think of the keepers who have walked up there before you. When I go up there I wonder, what did they see back then? What did they see in 1802? Were they doing the same thing I do? Watching the sun go down over Boston? Were they thinking the same thoughts? Did they know how lucky they were?"

"So when you talk about a presence, yeah I guess you can feel it. Then you look at this thing, this giant beacon, and you just say, wow."

"Having to go wind up the gears and oil the light, these guys loved this lighthouse. In going through some of the old photographs, there was a lot of pride there. I get that feeling now when I go up there. It's mine. You definitely feel that sense of pride in that it's yours to take care of. I feel honored that I'm in charge of this whole thing. I'm trusted with it. I take it as a great honor to do what I'm doing here. My goal is to get the public to share in it. To get the place open to the public."

Rick is a lighthouse keeper in a long line of keepers at Boston Light. He is doubtlessly entitled to his sense of awe. Someday, when he leaves, Rick will leave a part of his spirit here as well. At least, that is what he says he hopes will happen.

"I don't know if it's them that I feel or what it is, but there's definitely something out here, you know, a presence," he says in his pleasingly thick Boston accent.

But what about ghosts? I urge him. We've heard about hauntings on the island. Have you ever seen or heard anything that you thought was strange enough to be called a ghost?

"You hear all kinds of noises and bumps in the night in this building. You know, you really can't let your mind wander," he says, "although I do sometimes." He looks dead serious, but a smile is starting to grow from the corners of his eyes. And when it comes, it's accompanied by a hearty laugh. Rick is a likeable guy with a great sense of humor, but he takes his job very seriously. And you can't help feeling impressed by his dedication, his ability to endure the isolation of this light station.

Our conversation turns to George Worthylake, Boston Light's first keeper, and perhaps its first ghost. George arrived on the island on September 5, 1716. The new beacon had just been topped off and the light was being tested. Whale oil was the fuel of the day, and the powerful light burned lots of it. Several barrels were unloaded off the boat that brought George, his wife, and daughter to their new home.

The Worthylakes were a happy couple. Their daughter, although she suffered bouts of loneliness, adjusted to lighthouse living with few problems. Regular visits to the mainland helped her cope. It seemed that all three Worthylakes enjoyed occasional day trips to Boston, a treat Mr. Worthylake tried to arrange at least once a month.

On November 1, 1718, a little more than two years after they'd first stepped foot on the island, the Worthylakes woke up to the chill of a gray, foggy morning to their great disappointment. This was the day they had planned to travel to Boston for shopping and lunch, and perhaps a brief visit with their friends. The trip would have to be postponed. The Worthylakes' daughter was heartbroken.

By mid-morning, weather conditions improved slightly, but a

thick blanket of fog persisted, floating on top of the water. Visibility was poor and a light drizzle had commenced. Mrs. Worthylake told her husband she had a strange feeling about this trip, a sense of foreboding sweeping over her. But sensing how important this brief holiday was to their daughter, the couple decided to launch the small boat and head for the city.

The Worthylake family owned a slave named Shadwell. In every way George Worthylake trusted Shadwell, relying on the man not only for his physical strength, but for his intelligence and good judgement. We can only speculate, but perhaps Shadwell had his own doubts about a trip to Boston on this foul morning. Regardless of his misgivings, Worthylake gave the order, the boat was readied for the journey, and off they went into the harbor. As usual, Shadwell and Worthylake shared the rowing duties.

Their small boat sliced through the wet mist and they made good progress toward the city. The mood of the family was happy and expectant. But soon the fog grew thicker and the rain fell harder. At some point they must have known they were doomed. The Worthylakes and their slave, Shadwell, were never seen again. Months later their boat was discovered adrift, but their bodies were never found.

"I've heard several different ghost stories," says Rick Himelrich. "One story tells of a woman who appears out around the fog signal. She's in the shadows. Just a dark figure. And sometimes the fog horn goes off by itself. Now that I know that to be a fact."

"I also know people hear strange sounds out here at night. And people have reported hearing a name being called out. But I can't honestly say whose name it was they heard."

The wife of a keeper of Boston Light in the 1940s knows what she heard. She lived at the lighthouse with her husband and three children for two years, and she was not the first, nor the last, to sense a strange presence on the island. But the woman's story remains one of the most vivid. It started one day with the sound of footsteps following behind her on the beach. She turned around but no one was there. It happened two or three times, but only in the daylight, so it wasn't that scary. She told her oldest daughter it was nothing, but still she was rattled.

Then one night she grew terrified. She felt a presence in her bedroom. She was convinced someone was standing at her bedroom window—she saw the outline of a figure, a woman. But when she turned on the light, no one was there. She shook her husband awake, but he told her she must have been dreaming.

About a week later, in the middle of the night, she woke up to the sound of steady, maniacal laughter. She thought it was coming from the boathouse. The next night, she heard the laughter again. Somewhere under the heavy layers of hideous noise was the sound of sobbing—the desperate cries of a young girl. The woman couldn't make out what the girl was saying. It was someone's name. Over and over the girl cried out a name. But her thin voice was too muffled, too deeply buried in the laughter to make out the name.

The next night she heard the sobs again, but this time she also heard the name. She heard what the young girl had been crying. It was "Shadwell." The weak, frightened voice was crying, "Shadwell."

The keeper's wife made note of the date: it was the first day of November—the same day the Worthylakes had launched their boat in the fog and headed into tragedy. It was the date they disappeared forever.

Rick Himelrich tells us about an incident that occurred some decades ago in the lighthouse living quarters. He's uncertain about its connection to the Worthylakes. "One of the keepers was sitting in the living room of this building right here," pointing behind us to the keeper's dwelling. "The figure of a woman walked right by them. Plain as day. There were two gentlemen sitting there and they both saw her. She walked right by them."

"Whether there are ghosts out here or not..." he pauses and shrugs, shakes his head and smiles. "There was no woman at the lighthouse that day. At least not one who was a living, breathing human. Who was the woman? A ghost? Did they see a ghost out here? It's anybody's guess."

Could this woman be the spirit of Mrs. Worthylake, or perhaps her daughter? Hundreds of sudden, tragic deaths have occurred in these waters, on these islands in the shadow of this lighthouse. "There are three people whose ship wrecked on the island buried near the lighthouse," Rick says. "There's even a dog buried on this island, and a heck of a lot of sheep that drowned when they got caught in the tide."

John Forbes overhears Rick's last comment. "I don't know about any sheep, but a lot of the guys stationed out here have seen that woman," he says. "A woman who walks through the room. She's by herself. She comes in one door and walks out another. Or maybe it's a wall she walks through. But she never looks at anybody. Never says a word. Sounds like a ghost to me."

Rick is skeptical. He expresses his doubts, but then adds, "We had a snowstorm out here last winter. One of the keepers discovered footprints in the snow. They started nowhere and ended nowhere. They were just unexplained footprints. A man's boots."

Unlike Rick, John Forbes seems to readily accept the existence of a spirit world. "You're talking to someone who believes in ghosts. I believe in them a hundred percent," he says emphatically.

"In fact, I have a ghost in my own house. I strongly suspect he's a sea captain who used to live in the house. He comes to my room at night. Sometimes I kick at him, trying to keep him away. Can you imagine kicking at a ghost?" John laughs, but he's dead serious about the ghost. "Most of the time, as soon as I'm fully aware of him, he disappears anyway."

John lives on the mainland near the water in a neighborhood once populated with sailors who started in Boston Harbor and circled the globe. "I know this guy had a strong personality in life. Sometimes that's what it takes to become a ghost. He lived to a ripe old age, and when he died, they held his wake in the room where I see him. It's strange."

Boston Harbor is filled with strange tales, the mysterious islands and the historic Boston Lighthouse. Mysteries here seem to come from somewhere on the dark edges of the past, from secret places we might glimpse, never fully grasp; we will never know what lies beyond.

"Wherever you want to let your mind take you, it will. And it depends on what you want to believe," concludes Rick Himelrich.

T r a v e l   T i p s
Boston Light

Today you can reach Boston Light on Little Brewster Island by taking a National Park Service tour, which leaves from Boston, Thursday through Sunday mornings. The ticket for the boat trip and tour of the lighthouse also entitles you to a tour of the JFK Library in South Boston.

Boston Light

Little Brewster Island

Boston Harbor

John Forbes, the gentleman who shares his home with the ghost of a sea captain, claims to love the Red Parrot Restaurant in Hull. He says you can sit and enjoy dinner overlooking Nantasket Beach while you're admiring the lighthouse off in the distance.

Red Parrot Restaurant

Nantasket Beach

Hull, MA

www.theredparrot.com

—∾—

Jakes Seafood is another recommendation from the locals. We didn't make it to Jakes, but we heard about his postcard-covered walls from more than one person—a real conversation starter at Jakes. And the food's supposed to be great, too.

Jakes Seafood

Nantasket Beach

Hull, MA

—∾—

The crew and I had a memorable dining experience at the Nantasket Seafood Company, a rustic seafood restaurant on the water in Hull. It was one of the few times in New England that I ordered something other than lobster. Our waitress, who was friendly in a no-nonsense sort of way, suggested I try the swordfish—it had just come off the boat. The boat, as a matter of fact, was still sitting at the dock unloading while we ate. I've never tasted a fresher piece of fish.

To further endear us to the place, our audio grip was suffering from a dog bite. (No, not Sam, the Black Lab of Boston Light.) The poor guy was complaining of what he called an infected feeling. He ordered fish stew—big chunks of fresh halibut, shellfish, and vegetables in a clear, steaming broth. In minutes, he perked right up. I have no other evidence of this, but that fish stew seemed to have some medicinal value. So, take whatever ails you to the Nantasket Seafood Company and try the stew.

Nantasket Seafood Company

Nantasket Beach

Hull, MA

Haunted Eyes
Plymouth Lighthouse

Massachusetts

She was an old-fashioned lady. Out of place, as though she belonged to another time. Standing at the foot of the visitor's bed, her face like cold, white stone, her eyes the saddest he had ever seen. Was it a dream or was she a ghost? Where did she come from and what did she want?

America's oldest wooden lighthouse, built in 1768, sits alone and nearly forgotten on a skinny stretch of land at the entrance to Plymouth Bay. On a clear day from this spot you can practically see where the Pilgrims landed. Throughout the ages, from ancient times to early America, this ground has had a rich history. Many people believe it's beset by spirits as well.

Pilgrims called this peninsula Gurnet Point in honor of their homeland's favorite fish. But long before the Pilgrims appeared, the land was full of life. Native Americans hunted, fished, and buried their dead here, overlooking the bay. Artifacts identify the Gurnet as the site of one of North America's earliest settlements, dating back hundreds of years. Speculation has the lighthouse constructed directly over an ancient burial mound.

During the American Revolution, the Gurnet and the plain wooden lighthouse on its shore were of strategic importance to both sides. A British frigate went so far as to fire on the tower, trying to put out its light. A cannonball found its mark, splintered the wood and lodged in the side of the lighthouse, but the light wasn't damaged. It stayed on for the duration of the war.

Many old-timers believe Plymouth Lighthouse is protected by a power that can't be seen or explained. Locals from the neighborhood and visitors alike have claimed to feel a sense of strangeness when they venture near the light—not a scary feeling so much, just a dark, foreboding mood.

Photo by David Nowicki

Plymouth (Gurnet) Lighthouse, believed haunted by the
ghost of a woman who is known as "My Lady."

The first keeper at Plymouth Lighthouse was John Thomas, a local farmer who donated his land for its site. Tragically, soon after his appointment, John died of a mysterious illness. His widow, Hannah, took charge, but not much is known about her. It's been said that she performed the job admirably; she was strong, hard-working and utterly devoted to the lighthouse.

For two decades, Hannah kept the light burning. Then, after a brief illness, she also passed away. Supposedly her body was carted off and buried many miles inland. But following her death, certain eerie occurrences on the Gurnet led some people to suspect that a part of her never left—that her spirit remained behind.

Today, reaching Plymouth Lighthouse requires a four-wheel-drive vehicle and a strong stomach. It's a jarring five-mile journey across wild dunes and unruly beach grass to a hillside cluster of modest summer homes. Perched on a rise overlooking this quiet neighborhood, the white, wooden lighthouse sits unoccupied—abandoned except for the occasional visit of a U. S. Coast Guard crew. Although the light is operational, it's fully automated. And there may be some pretty strange things going on inside while it's supposed to be empty.

Some might call it negative energy, or at least peculiar energy. There's been talk in the community, so I was told, that during the summer season, neighborhood children steer clear of this place, choosing to keep their distance while playing and riding their bikes. Dogs and cats in the area have been seen skirting the property rather

U.S. Coast Guard photo

Plymouth (Gurnet) Lighthouse

than cutting across the yard as you'd expect from wandering animals. Among followers of such things, it's pretty well accepted that children and animals possess a greater sensitivity to the supernatural than the rest of us. There's nothing conclusive in any of this, of course, just speculation.

An elderly, gray-bearded fisherman from nearby Duxbury with a voice like a trumpet and a toothless smile told me in no uncertain terms he believes the lighthouse is haunted. Locals have heard sounds coming from the building, he said, at times when they know it's uninhabited, and all the doors and windows are locked. Shadowy movements have been glimpsed by passersby through dark windows.

No one has a clue about what's going on. But sometimes they whisper about spirits rising out of the ground like wisps of smoke, perhaps remnants from long-forgotten burial sites. No one has ever been harmed, and strangely nobody feels threatened—just a little uneasy sometimes.

Something strange appears to be gripping this lonely point of land. A nagging mystery hangs over it like a shroud of fog. Is it Hannah Thomas, the devoted lighthouse keeper? Or her husband who died suddenly before he could serve the beacon? Is it a calling from ancient Native America, or later in American history? No one can put a finger on who or what it is.

Talk of ghosts in New England is not unusual. People who dwell along this stretch of Massachusetts shoreline that curves gracefully northward to Boston from the Cape know a lot of ghost stories. It's in their air. Most of these coast dwellers know about the spooky wooden frame house on the Cape's north shore, built in 1790, located not too far from Plymouth Lighthouse. Residents of this house in Sandwich supposedly see the ghosts of young children running through the halls and up the stairs, appearing suddenly in dark corners, materializing in front of a fireplace only to disappear.

Footsteps are heard at all hours of the night in that house in Sandwich, and the apparition of an unidentified middle-aged man is said to haunt the third floor. Tragic events have plagued the house practically since it was built—including the owner's suicide in 1813 and his wife's mysterious disappearance. It's said that their seven frightened children remained alone in the house, forced to care for themselves. Are they the ghosts that people see today?

The coast of Massachusetts has known witches and demons and a whole legion of spirits inhabiting haunted mansions and inns. So, locals might not think that a haunted lighthouse in their midst is strange at all.

Several years ago, professional photographer Bob Shanklin was on assignment to capture a photograph of Plymouth Lighthouse at dawn. In order to help him prepare for the early photo shoot, he obtained permission for him and his wife, Sandra, to spend the night at this solitary light station.

It turned out to be one of the most fateful decisions of Bob's career. That night another woman entered his life, someone he came to call "my lady."

I heard Bob Shanklin's story in a roundabout way. One evening I telephoned Bob at his home in Fort Walton Beach, Florida. I had a hunch he could help. Bob and his wife Sandra are known as "the Lighthouse People." They're famous for having photographed every lighthouse in America. I found out later how exceptionally talented and well-traveled these people are.

The evening I called Bob I was chasing down rumors about lighthouse ghosts in the state's panhandle. A mutual friend had given me Bob's name.

"I don't know much about ghosts around here," declared Bob.

He sounded open and friendly and I liked him immediately. "Frankly, I don't think there's any truth to those stories in these parts," he added.

I thanked him and was about to hang up when he blurted out, "But I have my own lighthouse ghost story. I saw something you might call a ghost."

That night on the telephone, Bob told me one of the most spectacular ghost stories I had ever heard. And that's when it happened: I was hooked.

We settled on a date to meet in Plymouth, Massachusetts, the following month. Bob would go on-camera and talk about his strange experience. It had happened in the keeper's quarters at Plymouth Lighthouse, and that's where we'd do the interview.

Grabbing a camera and racing down to Florida to interview Bob at his home was a cheap and easy alternative to shooting on location. Always looking for ways to conserve my precious and limited budgets, I considered the former. But only for a moment. Hearing his story, even by telephone, was enough to convince me to reenact the experience in the keeper's house at Plymouth. His account of what he had seen sent a shiver up my spine. It was worth sharing that shiver with an audience, even though I knew the effort would present a challenge. And I never dreamed of just how big a challenge it would be.

Mid-April arrived right on schedule. I was excited, and so was my crew. I flew to Boston with the two guys and all our gear.

We rented a jeep, drove about sixty miles south to Plymouth, met Bob and his wife, and headed out to Gurnet Point. All without a hitch—so far.

Bouncing over the dunes in our jeep was a rugged experience, like white-water rafting on a bumpy stretch of dry land. We drove along Duxbury Beach on a road that frequently degenerated into two deep ruts through dark mounds of thick wet sand.

Pulling up outside the cottage, we could see the place was a wreck. Inside we discovered it was worse: holes in the ceiling, birds in the closets, rats in the basement—slimy, water-logged debris of unthinkable origin shoved into every corner. Welcome home.

Bob and Sandra couldn't believe this was the same place they had spent that night less than five years before.

We went back outside to investigate the lighthouse. Here in New England, they'd call it "quaint." Short in stature and constructed entirely of wood, even the fresh coat of white paint it was wearing couldn't make Plymouth Lighthouse look much more than homely. A lighthouse only a mother could love, someone remarked.

We climbed the low rise and approached the tower. The door was either locked or jammed. We jiggled it this way and that. Not the time to be too aggressive, I thought. Just being here was making me nervous. A charge of unlawful entry was all I needed. Nothing in the neighborhod was stirring, but were inquiring eyes peering out of shadowy windows? In this off-season afternoon, were the surrounding cottages really as abandoned as they appeared? One phone call by a concerned neighbor to the local authorities—or worse, to the Coast Guard—and the jig was up.

I was haunted by a question about our authorization to film at this location. Although I had made several calls to official places, and did receive some noncommittal "okays," there was nothing in my hand that resembled a permit. Our guide, a loquacious fellow from one of the local historical associations, possessed keys to the keeper's house, but not the lighthouse. This was as close to official as we got.

We didn't actually have our cars at the curb, engines running, but we were treading lightly, and prepared to leave in a hurry. It would not be the first time we had to vacate a venue quickly—or as they say, hot foot it out of there. But I wanted to do Bob's interview *here,* not in jail.

Back at the cottage, Bob led us down a gloomy hallway where white walls had turned dark yellow and a strong musty odor burned the back of our throats. We discovered the room where Bob had had his encounter with—with what? The *unknown?* The room was empty except for a dozen or so sheets of plywood stacked against one wall. Apparently someone had once considered fixing this place up, then had a better idea and never came back.

Otherwise the room was just as Bob had described it, with a single window in the wall opposite the door looking out at the light-house, which stood only a few yards away. Our cameraman and audio grip dragged a rusted metal bed frame into the room. A spongy damp mattress came in next, followed by a wobbly kitchen chair. "Isn't this called dumpster diving?" I asked. They finessed the bed into the precise spot Bob remembered. "A little to the right, no, a little to the left," Bob was directing.

Next, the two guys went off in search of a source of power to run the camera lights. The camera will run on batteries but the lights require electricity to operate. Because the day was heavily overcast, and the room's one window was deep in late-afternoon shadows, we were going to need plenty of artificial light to cast on Bob.

This time the guys returned in minutes, empty-handed, heads shaking, looking about as bleak as our surroundings. I braced myself for the bad news—no power. Furthermore, the gasoline generator promised by our guide wouldn't run a miniature flashlight much less our rack of TV lights.

We interviewed Bob in a pretty dark room. Not pitch dark, understand, just muddy. The video image suffered, became too grainy. But after all, this is a ghost story. (Much later I grew fond of characterizing our light as moody, and acting as though we'd planned to shoot it that way.)

The crew took up their positions with camera and audio gear, Bob reclined on the spongy bed, a little squeamishly at first. I teetered as noiselessly as possible in the broken-down chair. And finally, the camera rolled.

What happened next was close to magic. Suddenly nothing else in the room mattered. Bob's voice dropped to a low, scratchy whisper, his brow furrowed in concentration, his eyes glazed over as if they were seeing things unseen by the rest of us. We forgot about the musty smell, the spiders and—except for an occasional cooing—the birds in the closet. We slipped under the storytelling spell of Bob Shanklin.

He began by setting the scene. It was already dark, well past dinner time on a winter night. "It was a chilly evening," he recalled, "and I can remember the wind blowing quite strong. We were very tired. Sandra was in bed beside me. She had fallen off to sleep. Sometime during the night I woke up here in the bed and sat up watching the window light."

Bob described the light. It was pure white, and the beacon's intermittent flashes filled the dark room with bursts of brilliant illumination. For some people the effect might have been unsettling. For Bob, it was hypnotic.

"I was just about in the position I'm in now," he said, leaning back on the side of the bed closest to the window.

"The window would light up then go completely dark, light, then dark. For a while I couldn't take my eyes off it. Then I happened to glance over at Sandra."

That's when he saw the person—the strange woman—standing over his wife. How could there be someone else in the room. Something wasn't right. A moment before, Bob was sure he had been alone with his wife. Now there was another woman. Who was she? The hair on Bob's neck stood up.

Photo by Joseph Schiffbauer

*Actress in TV film Haunted Lighthouses portrays "My Lady," a
ghost who haunts the keeper's bedroom*

"I noticed this lady, maybe eighteen inches away from Sandra's face, and she had come out of nowhere." Just as Bob finished his sentence, he jerked his head around to look at the spot where the lady had been standing. The mattress shook, the springs squealed, and we all jumped about a foot in the air.

"My lady" is what Bob named the uninvited visitor—just a name that popped into his head at that moment. She was a woman in her mid-thirties, Bob estimated. She was tall and bony thin, dressed in a plain, old-fashioned housecoat, her dark brown hair falling around her shoulders. The color of her skin was more milky white than pale. Her face was lined with deep blue veins, her cheekbones were like wax. I imagine a zombie standing rigidly over the bed.

She looked like someone who had suffered from a long illness, Bob remembered, or someone who was dead. Shudder.

"I looked at her and she looked at me, and the only thing I could concentrate on was her eyes," Bob said in a hushed tone. "Her eyes were the saddest things I had ever seen."

Bob had his eyes riveted on her. She stared back, not blinking or smiling. Neither of them moving a muscle.

"My first reaction was—how did she get here, who is she, what is she? But I didn't feel like she was out of place in this room. It was like she belonged. And maybe I was the intruder.

Bob was seeing the woman by the light of the flashing beacon. When the light flashed off, Bob could feel her continuing to stare—as though she could see him in the dark.

"As I looked at her, I could see the window light up then go dark, just out of the corner of my eye. It was either the fourth or fifth time the window lit up that I glanced toward it, away from her. When I glanced back, she was gone."

"All the contact we had was through our eyes. Her eyes spoke of a sad loneliness. But they were riveting. I've never met anyone with eyes that magnetic—you couldn't help but be drawn to her eyes and be held by them."

He isn't sure who this lady might have been, or even if she was real. But Bob claims he's tormented by what might have been. "What could have happened between us if I hadn't been distracted by the flashing light and looked away?" Bob mused about a conversation he might have had with her, questions he wished he could have posed. "I wanted her back. I wanted to ask her who she was, where she had come from. I never had the chance. I feel bad that I looked away when I did. I wonder if I hadn't glanced toward the window she may have spoken to me. I can't get that out of my mind.

"I think there are a lot of things that happen in our world that we can't explain. This was one of them. I have many, many more questions than I have answers."

As near as anyone can tell, Hannah Thomas, widow of the first keeper and lighthouse keeper herself for almost twenty years, slept each night right here in this room, or a room just like it next to the tower.

Could Bob's lady be the ghost of Hannah Thomas—a ghost who continues to possess her former quarters in the keeper's house? Does her lingering spirit swirl around this space like smoke inside a bottle, in constant motion, unable to find its way out? Or could My Lady be someone else entirely?

"We did some research and found that there was another lady who lived here after Hannah Thomas died. She and her husband kept the lighthouse back in the mid 1800s."

This was a devoted couple, according to what Bob discovered. One day the man went out in the ocean in a small boat on a rescue mission, and in a swell the boat capsized and sank. Soon after her husband's body washed ashore, the heartsick widow died in her sleep.

"She probably died in this room. I kind of wondered if she was My Lady. And with my beard, did I resemble her husband? Is that why she was staring at me?"

A history of tragedy and death are nothing new to Gurnet Point. "There have been countless shipwrecks in the area," Bob declared. "The pilgrims landed only a few miles behind us; the whole area is steeped in history. My Lady has to fit into it some-place."

"When they did excavation work out here they found traces of the Norsemen under the lighthouse. Where we are sitting right now was a Native American cemetery. It gives you a lot to think about."

"I got the feeling she was looking for something. I feel certain that she'll visit someone else someday."

Bob insisted that he never saw a ghost in his life—until that night. "I know it wasn't a dream. I know I was wide awake. I made it a point to let myself know I wasn't dreaming.

"I didn't say anything about it to my wife until the next morning. Sandra was disappointed I didn't wake her up. I told her My Lady's face was only a couple of feet away from her own. I didn't want Sandra waking up and having the experience of seeing some lady's face that close. I thought it might be a little too frightening for her."

"But for me, I think I was blessed to see this woman, whoever she was. It was a gift that most people never have the chance to experience."

I asked Bob if he thought that seeing this lady was like a glimpse of another world—or into another dimension. Perhaps she was standing at a doorway, between two dimensions?

"Maybe she was," he says with a touch of melancholy. "I don't know. I just got the feeling she was here especially for me, and I'll live with that memory for the rest of my life."

He doesn't like to use the word *ghost* to describe her. "I kind of hate to hear her called that. I always thought that ghosts were scary," he chuckles." But she wasn't scary, she wasn't spooky. She was just a sad lady."

The little slice of daylight that had been spilling through the window had waned, and so had Bob. The crew was bushed and I felt mentally exhausted. The intensity of this interview had taken its toll.

We moved about lethargically, packing up the camera gear and quietly preparing to head home. It was strange—wrapping up a day's work without the usual banter and jokes. Our silence spoke volumes about our emotions.

I will not forget the experience we shared that afternoon, or Bob Shanklin himself, for that matter. With his snow white beard, black Greek fisherman's cap, and chilling account set at the bleak cottage out on Gurnet Point, Bob made an impression, and the memory will haunt me forever.

But as Bob might remind us, it isn't really a ghost story, just a story about a sad lady.

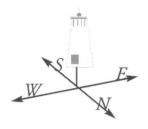

Travel Tips
Plymouth Lighthouse

If you've read the story about the sad lady at Plymouth Lighthouse, you're already aware that reaching Gurnet Point is quite an undertaking. In addition to the obstacles mentioned in the story, our local guide warned us the road washes out unpredictably, and there are no public tours of the lighthouse. The *No Trespassing* sign is hard to miss. Discouraged yet?

If you're a die-hard adventurer who simply must see America's oldest wooden lighthouse—one that might be haunted by a very enchanting ghost—gas up your four-wheeler and head north out of Plymouth on Route 3. Watch for signs to Duxbury. Turn onto Route 3A in the direction of Duxbury Beach. The beach road heads straight south into Plymouth Bay.

On your map you'll see a thin peninsula, barely a filament of land, shaped, if you stretch your imagination, like a skinny hockey stick. That's Duxbury Beach, and at its southernmost tip is Gurnet Point. Follow the road until you can't go any farther.

You'll see the lighthouse on a grassy rise.

Friends of Plymouth Light hopes to raise enough money to open the lighthouse to the public someday. That hasn't happened yet—so even if you brave the trip, you'll have to settle for a drive-by.

> Not open to the public
> Friends of Plymouth Light
> 21 Wampatuk Road
> Scituate, MA 02066

—∞—

Spirits can be what you make them, and sometimes places steeped in history have a distinctly spiritual feel. Plymouth is one of them, and it's packed with historical tourist attractions, starting with Plymouth Rock. You can see most of them on your own. But here's a suggestion about how to enhance your sightseeing experience. A memorable history tour of Plymouth is offered by Colonial Lantern Tours. And it's a winner. With knowledgeable guides, you'll enjoy the original plantation site and details you may otherwise miss—like walking through a fascinating early American cemetery. Go at night and they'll lend you a pierced-tin lantern to help light your way. It's one of the best tours anywhere.

> Colonial Lantern Tours
> 800-698-5636
> www.lanterntours.com

My advice on lodging in Plymouth—unless you absolutely have to stay downtown, don't. It's crowded, in many cases overpriced, and parking is a nightmare. Get out and enjoy the countryside and a whole host of wonderful inns, B&Bs, and motels. (I made the worst possible choice of accommodations, right in the heart of Plymouth, so I speak with experience.) For Plymouth tourist information: www.visit-plymouth.com.

A recommendation from our guide is a charming B&B on Route 3, at Exit 2, one exit south of Plymouth. Seagate Farm has rooms available with private en suite baths and ocean views. Eleven acres invite roaming and a private beach on which to stroll. A New England country breakfast is included—lobster quiche is a famous specialty. It's moderately expensive, no pets, no smoking. Children over 10 are permitted.

Seagate Farm
296 Center Hill Road
Plymouth, MA 02360
1-888-BNB-1620
www.seagatefarm.com

On the edge of town, two miles from Plymouth Harbor, you'll find a handsome colonial B&B with a direct ocean view, another recommendation of our local guide. Bedrooms and suites at Thorton Adams House all have private baths, phones, and air conditioning. Prices are moderate, and a hearty country breakfast is included.

Thorton Adams House

73C Warren Avenue

Plymouth, MA 02360

888-747-9700

www.thortonadams.com

—∞—

A motel with a surprising variety of accommodations, especially good for families and groups traveling together, about 6 miles from downtown Plymouth on Route 3A, is called The Blue Spruce. We met people staying here who raved about all the space they had for their family to spread out. It offers your choice of one-bedroom townhouses and two-bedroom cottages. Some have a patio, phone, microwave, and coffeemaker. All rooms have a refrigerator and combo shower/bath. Prices are moderate.

The Blue Spruce Motel

710 State Street

Plymouth, MA

800-370-7080

—∞—

The hostelries mentioned above are not haunted—at least I don't think they are. Disappointed? Perhaps you haven't reached your quota of ghosts while visiting haunted lighthouses, so permit me to recommend something more suitable—something supernatural.

From Plymouth to Cape Cod is spitting distance, some Yankees will tell you, but that would be in a world without summer traffic jams. Off season you might just make it to Hyannisport from Plymouth in under an hour—in high season add another hour.

Once there it's your choice of the Cape's hundreds of perfectly charming inns and B&Bs. But I'm here to tell you about a perfectly haunted one. Oh, it's charming, too, but for more than sixty years now, Simmons Homestead Inn in Hyannisport has been the home of a pretty little seven-year-old girl—who just happens to be a ghost. She's friendly, although a bit mischievous, and her name is Susan.

The Simmons Homestead Inn is handsome—a classic example of early nineteenth century Greek Revival. Built in 1820 by a young sea captain, Lemuel Simmons, it changed hands several times, and in the early 1900s became the home of the Lombard family. Late one summer afternoon, the Lombard's youngest granddaughter wandered too close to the still waters of Simmons pond behind the house. She slipped, fell into the murky pond, and drowned.

"Before I bought this building in 1988, I had never seen, nor did I believe in ghosts," current owner William Putnam told me in a telephone conversation we had one evening. "But I do feel a presence here—I feel Susan. I've seen fleeting images and heard her giggling."

Putnam told me the ghost is about four feet tall, wears a long white dress, and she giggles a lot. Room Number Five of the inn was formerly Susan's bedroom. Many guests who have stayed in that room have come to breakfast with chilling stories. But she won't hurt you—according to Putnam, no one who has visited the inn has gone away frightened of Susan.

This cozy, two-story inn has fourteen comfortable guest rooms, some with canopied beds, fireplaces, and unique decor. Rates vary according to season.

Simmons Homestead Inn
288 Scudder Avenue
Hyannisport, MA 02647
508-778-4999/800-637-1649

Incidentally, Bob Shanklin, who is featured in this chapter, and his wife, Sandra, are both photographers living in Fort Walton Beach, Florida. Several books of their work have been published.

The Lighthouse People
850-862-4069
www.thelighthousepeople.com

A Deadly Melody
Seguin Island Lighthouse

Maine

Isolation can be deadly—wrecking hopeful lives, ruining happy marriages, and driving sensible people to commit unspeakable acts.

A lonely lighthouse, a foggy night, an isolated island off the coast of Maine—these are the makings of a nightmare.

Seguin Island Lighthouse, off the coast of Maine.

Impact Television Photo

A glance at a map might tell you the boat ride from the Maine coast to Seguin Island is a routine experience. After all, it's only about three miles from the safe harbor of Popham Beach to the island's rocky shore. But anyone who has made the trip will testify it's far from smooth sailing. Even when the weather is ideal, swift currents swirling around in choppy waters can make the journey a hair-raising experience. And when weather conditions turn nasty, the crossing becomes downright hazardous. Lives have been lost attempting it.

"You have to pass through this stretch where the Kennebec River meets the sea," warns Charter Boat Captain, Howie Marston.

"It's some of the East Coast's choppiest water." Marston plows these waters in his sturdy craft, *Old Duff*, and knows Seguin like the back of his hand.

Another person who knows a great deal about Seguin Island is author and lighthouse historian Elinor De Wire. Her book, *Guardians of the Lights,* is one of the finest introductions to lighthouses ever written. She even includes a chapter on haunted lighthouses. But when it comes to ghosts, Elinor is a skeptic. "Let's just say these are legends and they are meant to be fun," she declares.

Maine's coast is dotted with lighthouses, and most have legends attached to them. Some tales are bloodcurdling stories about scary things that crawl out of dark corners to give you the creeps. Then there are other accounts—stories of friendly spirits that help people through perilous times.

When storms blow over Boothbay Harbor, just a few miles north of Seguin, mariners report distant fog whistles and lights glowing on the rocky shoreline near Ram Island Light. But there is no glowing beacon here—no light and no whistle. Legend has it the lights and whistles are warning signals given by the spirit of a dead seaman. He froze to death on these shores some two hundred years ago after a storm sent his boat crashing onto the rocks. He's a good spirit, though—presumably protecting his fellow sailors.

Farther north near Rockland, Maine, boaters have reported seeing an old keeper at the top of Owls Head Lighthouse. Of course, there is no lightkeeper at Owls Head, and there hasn't been one here for decades. During the winter season, when frequent snowstorms cover the island in a white blanket, visitors to Owls Head have discovered large boot prints—prints that lead to the lighthouse and keeper's quarters. Nobody knows what this specter is up to, whether he's a friendly ghost, or an evil spirit. Since many sightings have been recorded, something must be going on.

Sudden death seems to produce ghosts. That's a given among the paranormal experts who make this sort of judgement. Raging storms and shipwrecks are often connected to the existence of lingering spirits as well. But how about loneliness? Some people will tell you lonely places can be as devastating to the soul as the most violent killer storms. And Seguin Island Lighthouse is as lonely a place as you can imagine.

"Seguin is a lighthouse that is very close to shore yet it might as well be a million miles away," Elinor says. She has visited Seguin many times and knows how an empty feeling of isolation on this lonely island can creep up on you.

Centuries ago, Native Americans named the island Seguin. It meant "a little spit in the sea" in their language. From a distance it looks like a bulging hump of rock—a giant stone whale. French explorer Champlain compared its shape to that of a huge turtle. A haven for seagulls and migratory birds, the island is spotted with off-white droppings that decorate its cliffs like abstract art.

At the western edge of the sixty-four acre rock island rises a lofty white beacon, towering 180 feet above the Atlantic. This is the highest and most powerful lighthouse in Maine—and one of the oldest.

"It was George Washington himself who commissioned Seguin Island Lighthouse," explains Philip Jermain, president of Friends of Seguin Island, a non-profit group dedicated to preserving this historic site. "That was in 1792. Three years later it was completed— at a whopping $6300—a cost that staggered many people at the time."

It turned out to be a good investment. The lighthouse has been guarding the entrance to one of Maine's busiest waterways ever since.

The U.S. Lighthouse Board, which in those days governed all American aids to navigation, identified Seguin Lighthouse as "one of the most important positions on the eastern coast." Seguin Island was a strategic naval site in the War of 1812. A battle between the U.S. *Enterprise* and the British *Boxer* took place off Seguin's coast. During World War II, the island was a vital watch point for submarines.

Not only is this isolated location strategically important, it can be breathtakingly beautiful. Through the ages, Seguin has even been considered inspirational.

Years ago a famous Maine poet, Robert Tristam Coffin, loved to gaze out to the island from his home in Bath. He wrote, "At one gap in the high laces of the firs, on a clear night, I would see the star of Seguin, and in the fog mulls I could hear Seguin's foghorn lowing

. . . all through my dreams."

Adjoining the lighthouse is a gray, wood frame, two-story building with a wide front porch, blue-shuttered windows, and a red-brick chimney—typical nineteenth-century New England architecture. This was the place many generations of lighthouse keepers called home.

Most of the year, Seguin is wracked by storms or wrapped in fog. For more than two centuries, under these extreme conditions, the beacon has been a lifesaver for hundreds of ships. Without the lighthouse, the surrounding sea would be a gruesome burial ground for a legion of unlucky mariners. As it is, many ships have wrecked in neighboring waters.

At least one of the vessels that went down near Seguin was a pirate ship. Legend tells us that the pirate drowned, but not before he had hidden his treasure chest among the giant rocks. Many adventurers have tried their luck at finding the treasure, and some still believe it's here—a fortune in gold and silver coins buried somewhere on one of the steep cliffs.

Consider yourself forewarned: they say the treasure is guarded by the pirate's ghost. His horrid curse will fall upon your head if you so much as touch his precious treasure trove.

But legends and fog are not the only thing that enshroud this mysterious island. And they're a trifle compared to bloody murder.

A horrible tragedy occurred here sometime in the 1850s. As Elinor De Wire explains, "There's a delicious story about a couple who lived out there. We don't have any specific dates, we don't have any names, but we have lots of people who tell different versions."

One clear February day, a tall, good-looking young man wearing a dark blue uniform proudly sailed into the sheltered harbor of Seguin Island, a beautiful young woman at his side. The man was the new lighthouse keeper and she was his bride. The former keeper had died suddenly, and the new man had been selected to take over at the remote beacon. With arms linked tightly together, the young couple stood smiling at the front of the small boat as it sailed carefully up to the wooden dock.

In those days, it happened that the job of lighthouse keeper at such a remote station was not an easy position to fill. And the downside of service on Seguin was legendary. Out here in the Atlantic, the wind roars, the birds scream, and punishing waves echo as they beat the rocky shore. The torment is enough to rattle the heartiest soul. Nature bestowed the harshest conditions on Seguin, and the island was unforgiving.

Even the foghorn was known to wreak havoc. When the fog rolled in, as it did on most nights, the signal roared with blasts so strong that seabirds in its path were knocked down by the force.

Strangely, this charming young couple seemed pleased to be here. Remote? They scoffed at the suggestion. Bleak winter landscapes couldn't phase these love-blind newlyweds. The woman was swept away by the handsome keeper, and he was thrilled by his lovely bride. The prospect of a honeymoon on this island hideaway was deeply romantic. Blissfully they strolled up the long wooden ramp that led from the rocky beach to the lighthouse high on a cliff. They giggled at their good fortune, unaware that wisps of cold fog were already rolling across the flat gray sky.

By accident, the woman's steamer trunk slipped off a cart and hit the ground, popping open to reveal its contents. Feathered hats and party dresses spilled out onto the brown pebbly beach.

"I don't think she had any idea what she was about to encounter," Elinor De Wire comments. "She probably looked at the island and said, 'that's not far away, I can get home, go to church, visit my family.' But reality is, fall, winter, early spring, you just don't get off Seguin."

Connie Small, whose husband Elson tended the light on Seguin from 1926 to 1930, recalls that the island was infested with snakes that fed on rats living under the dock. She remembers the droning foghorn and how nerve-wracking it was when you couldn't get away from the sound.

"You take a delicate young person from the mainland and put them out on a place like that," Connie cringes, "it would be a sin to do it, really it would. I can see where some people could lose their minds."

Few brides just beyond their teens are cut out for isolation, and it didn't take long for Seguin Island to start getting under the young woman's skin. Interminable mornings were followed by long, lonely afternoons. She tried to fill the empty hours with writing letters and

Impact Television Photo

Actors in the TV film Haunted Lighthouses portray a happy couple arriving on Seguin Island before tragedy strikes, leaving the lighthouse haunted by the tune of a ghostly piano.

reading books. It worked for awhile, but there was never enough to do. She'd kill time by standing on a ledge high above the water, staring down at the rocks and roiling sea below, becoming giddy and unbalanced. *Just like my life*, she thought.

On rare days when the fog lifted, she stared wistfully across the water at the little town of Popham. Once her home, it was now just a smudge on the dark horizon. The sounds of birds and crashing waves and bleating foghorn all conspired to assault her eardrums like a sharp knife.

Her husband's job at the lighthouse was no comfort for her. He often worked from dawn until midnight. When he wasn't up top polishing the brass, he was down below in the engine house oiling and tinkering. Too much time to think made her thoughts turn bitter and disturbed. *His romance is no longer with me, but with his damnable lighthouse,* she lamented.

Suzie Perow lives on the mainland today, but she spent one summer living alone at the lighthouse. During that time she became convinced that island life is not meant for everyone.

"This type of isolation for some people might be what they are looking for, something that brings them to grace," says Suzie. "But for some people it might be what brings them to the edge of losing their minds."

The young keeper's wife was surely approaching the edge, and her husband must have sensed it. Desperate to help her, he concocted a plan. He would arrange to have a piece of the mainland conveyed to the island, thereby comforting his wife and quelling her homesickness.

He waited for a calm day, went ashore, and with the help of some Popham Beach residents, hauled back to the island a huge wooden crate. Winches, pulleys and strong arms served to hoist the heavy box up the steep ramp to the house. He believed what was in this box had the power to end his wife's misery and heal their broken marriage.

The young woman missed her music, that much he knew. On the mainland, music had been her passion. What could please her more than having a piano on the island? He was right, she was delighted. She danced around in the keeper's house like a happy child on Christmas morning. Then she sat down to play.

"She didn't want to be out on Seguin," declares Suzie Perow. "She didn't want to be away from the world. And the piano was her connection to the world."

Night fell. In the candlelit parlor the keeper's wife sat at her new piano and played furiously. She played as though she were chasing the demons—chasing them from her house, her mind, her life. Outside, the weather turned ugly. Curly wisps of thick fog began to creep in from the sea. Soon the island was lost in a soupy wet blanket of fog. But the young woman played her song, oblivious to whatever was happening outside.

"The one problem with this piano was that it had only one piece of sheet music in it," explains Elinor De Wire. "And this was a woman who couldn't improvise very well. So she ended up playing this one song—over and over again."

"She was wrapped up in that one little tune," Connie Small observes. "That tune is what was helping her exist."

Miserable, thick fog swallowed the house, hanging like a gray curtain around the entire island. The woman continued to play. She played the one song she knew, again and again, working herself into a frenzy. She played in defiance of the dreadful screeching birds, droning foghorn, and crashing waves.

"She was now playing at all hours of the night," Elinor explains. "On and on this infernal song went. So you can imagine her poor husband trying to cope with this and realizing his wife was slowly but surely going insane."

Without food or sleep, the woman began to look deathly pale and haggard. The keeper, too, was losing his grip—and his patience. He couldn't hide from the hellish racket. She played with wild abandon, as though she were trying to kill him with her song. *This song is her revenge,* thought the keeper. The music followed him into the engine house, it echoed inside the tower. Once he feared for his wife's sanity—now he feared for his own.

The man crept into the parlor soundlessly—not that she could have heard him over her piano. But something caught her eye. Above her head, she saw the angry glint of an ax, the sharp blade poised to cut through the air. She stiffened her neck and braced herself for the blow. The music stopped. Her blood spilled down over the ivory keys and dripped into a crimson puddle on the pinewood floor.

Possessed by rage, the keeper swung his ax like a scythe, cutting deeply into everything in its path—his wife, the piano. He struck at least a hundred times before he bolted for the cold iron stairs, up to his dark refuge at the top of the lighthouse. Alone in the watchroom, he stood staring into the honeycombed lens. It distorted his image like a funhouse mirror. His eyes bulged like a monster's, his face rippled over and over in the stacks of glass prisms.

He laughed at what he saw—he laughed until he heard something that gripped him with fear. He jerked his head around and peered down the winding staircase toward the room below. Fear became anger—once again, his rage began to grow. What he heard was the single note of a piano—then a tune. It was her song drifting up from the keeper's cottage. The piano was in pieces—pieces scattered with those of his wife. But he heard her song—drifting up the tower to possess him like a curse from the dead. He had to stop this echo inside his head.

By morning the fog had lifted and all was peaceful on Seguin Island. Alarmed to see the lighthouse dark, a group of mainlanders rowed out to the island to investigate. They found the keeper first. At the base of the tower, his mangled body lay in a lifeless heap, his face frozen in terror.

What they encountered in the cottage was the work of the devil himself—worse than any nightmare: the young woman hacked by a madman, shards of smashed piano strewn across the room, a bloody ax.

Shocked beyond belief, the mainlanders wondered what could drive a person to commit such a horrid act—then jump from the tower to his own death.

The men rowed back to their homes, reported the scene to the authorities, and told their wives and families about the horror they had discovered on Seguin Island.

Months passed and a new lighthouse keeper was appointed. The man moved out to the island and settled in the lighthouse dwelling.

It wasn't long before the keeper noticed something very strange happening around the lighthouse. On certain evenings when the wind was just right, he thought he heard music coming from somewhere on the island.

People on the mainland began to hear unusual stories from lobstermen who laid their traps in the waters of Seguin. Making their way back to port on foggy nights, what they heard coming from the island couldn't be explained.

A local lobsterman sporting a curly white beard and shiny yellow slicker agreed to speak to me about what he has heard in the waters of Seguin. He suspects there are others who could come forward—but won't. He's retired now and unmistakably Maine, his accent as thick as chowder. As he spoke he shot furtive glances from side to side and kept his voice low.

"I'd be cruising back into port about nine or ten o'clock at night, tired and a little edgy from a long day out on the water. Passing Seguin there'd be this faint music just drifting over my boat—a piano, I believe. It just wavered in and out, a little like the wind. But it was always the same tune. Got so I'd expect it—even listen for it sometimes. Then one day I found out there was nobody playing a piano on that island. That kind of spooked me."

The ghost of the woman who was murdered by her husband—if that is the ghost people hear—is not a frightful wraith or vengeful spirit as you might expect. Locals will tell you her spirit remains on the island to make sure we don't forget what life was like out there—out on a lonely station like Seguin. Her tragic story is a reminder of how difficult it is to live on an isolated island, and how some people don't cope with solitude very well.

Like most lighthouses today, the beacon on Seguin is automated. There is no keeper on the island and, of course, no piano. But on certain nights when the breeze is just right, you, too, might hear an eerie melody drifting from the solitary cottage. Listen to her song and remember that poor young woman who was murdered in her parlor. Listen to her song and let the past come back to life.

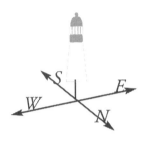

Travel Tips
Seguin Island Lighthouse

The smooth white tower and glossy black lantern stand at only fifty-three feet, but the effect is striking, a little intimidating, in fact. The huge optic has a lot to do with it—a first-order Fresnel lens, its lower prisms visible from the ground. It's a massive glass structure. By day it sparkles in the sun; by night it's blinding in its brilliance.

Topped off and first lighted in 1857, the beacon is still active today. The attached one-and-a-half story, red brick keeper's quarters was first occupied during that year. Originally a wooden lighthouse, constructed in 1795, stood on the island. It blew down in a fierce windstorm in 1819.

A small, white brick building is nearly hidden at the edge of the island. People in the know skirt around this structure like it's full of spiders. What's in it won't kill you, but it's practically that dangerous, and signs are posted to warn visitors to keep clear. This is the fog signal house. The awesome horn, a trumpeting sound intended to penetrate the fog and travel many miles, can deafen you at close range.

Ear-piercing foghorn blasts might be the only real hazard, but it's not the only warning that will be issued here. Aside from the tune that fishermen hear playing on the breeze, a whole raft of ghosts have been seen and heard on Seguin Island. According to William O. Thomson in his book *The Ghosts of New England Lighthouses,* lighthouse keepers he has talked to have spotted a young girl running up and down the cottage stairs. She has been known to wave to the men, and sometimes they hear her laughing as she goes. Another sound people report hearing in the cottage is a bouncing ball coming from an upstairs bedroom. Of course, there's never anyone with a ball upstairs when the sound is heard.

Another apparition that Thomson includes in his story about Seguin is an old sea captain. Apparently he has been seen many times climbing the iron stairs leading up to the watchroom. And he makes himself right at home in the lighthouse.

Just consider it a heads up. When you visit the island, you may want to be on alert.

Seguin Island Light
Friends of Sequin Island
P.O.Box 866
Bath, Maine
207-442-7055

Seguin Island Lighthouse

—𝔪—

Seguin Island is off the Maine coast from the town of Bath, which is north of Portland. Maine's coast is an irregular shoreline made up of a series of rocky points and appendages. Imagine fingerlike peninsulas dangling into the Gulf of Maine to form a bizarre-looking skeletal hand. At the top of one of these fingers, on the western shore of the Kennebec River, is Bath, founded by shipbuilders in the early 1600s. That's where you're headed.

To reach Bath, travel north on I-95 from Portland, taking care not to follow I-495 north which heads inland. It's a common mistake. Travel I-95 to the Brunswick exit, where you pick up Route 1 heading east.

In Bath, consider a stop at the Maine Maritime Museum & Shipyard where you'll discover fascinating information about the region. Pick up a schedule for the Museum's river cruise to Seguin Island, then take some time to explore the interesting array of marine exhibits. You can call ahead for cruise information and schedule if you prefer.

Maine Maritime Museum & Shipyard
Bath, Maine
207-443-1316

—𝔪—

Be prepared for a surprisingly steep, downhill journey on Route 209 from Bath to Popham Beach, about twenty miles or so. The two-lane road winds around like a serpent. About halfway down to

Popham, on your right-hand side, check out the old-fashioned country store famous for having just about everything you can imagine needing for your vacation—all crammed into a compact space about the size of a standard convenience store. Provisions for every occasion—camping, boating, wearing, eating—whatever your pleasure. As usual, diligent in our preparation for every conceivable emergency, we stocked up on Mountain Dew, candy bars, and chips.

When you approach the scenic shoreline, the road begins to twist wildly, teasing you into expecting an eyeful of blue water around every turn. Finally, there it is, a stunning finale to your drive. Popham's deep harbor fills your windshield with blue.

If for some reason you choose not to take the Bath Museum boat trip to Seguin Island, preferring to explore independently, a charter boat is for hire at Popham Beach. During the Seguin location shooting of *Haunted Lighthouses*, we used Kennebec Charters to haul cast, crew, and cameras over to the island. Captain Howie Marston, owner of the company, is delightful company and a terrific skipper. No two trips were the same. On one crossing he pointed out baby seals splashing about the harbor, on another outing he showed us a rarely-seen family of osprey at work building a nest on the island's rocky shore.

Howie's charter boat, *Old Salt*, is available for sightseeing, fishing and island hopping, at what seemed to me a reasonable hourly rate, especially if you're hauling four or five people.

Kennebec Charters

Popham Beach, Maine

207-389-1883

—∞—

Trivia buffs, did you know the first English attempt to colonize New England occurred right here at Popham Beach? Look across from the dock and check out the ruins of Fort Popham. Its construction was started in 1861, but oddly enough the fort was never completed. These dark, craggy ruins are spooky enough to have their own volume of eerie ghost tales.

—∞—

I was enchanted with a café in Bath called Kristina's—a beautifully renovated white frame house on hilly residential Centre Street. Three small dining rooms downstairs and a larger one upstairs are staffed by a friendly, energetic crew and supported by a kitchen that creates simple yet intriguingly delicious dishes. The prices at Kristina's are reasonable, portions large, and quality high. Plates are imaginatively presented. In the foyer a glass case just about bursts with luscious cakes and pastries. Leaving empty-handed is impossible. The shady front porch is open for lunch, weather permitting. We enjoyed several meals here and one day had Kristina's cater lunch out to the island. It's highly recommended.

Kristina's

Centre Street

Bath, Maine

Returning late one night from the island in a dense fog, Howie Marston's boat, *Old Salt,* was cutting through curtains of heavy mist as fast as she could travel. But it appeared we were going to arrive after the last restaurant was shuttered. We were like a crew of hungry and grumpy fishermen. The hour was nearing eleven, it was a weeknight, off season. Spinneys came to the rescue. If I describe Spinneys, I might scare you away. Just go. It's rustic to a fault, but fresh lobster and other local seafood gets cooked up in their kitchen to perfection. If they have fresh cod on the menu, order it. Spinneys, located on the dock at Popham Beach, is very casual, reasonably priced, and very, very good.

Spinneys

On the dock

Popham Beach, Maine

The *Popham Beach Bed and Breakfast* is *the* place to stay in Popham Beach. I didn't spend much time in the room—we worked out on the island day and night—but I sure remember the view: gentle waves lapping at the dune; soft muted foghorn humming in the distance; salty ocean air you taste with every breath. It was pure Maine seacoast.

The gray clapboard structure, formerly a Coast Guard station, was recently converted into an inn by Peggy Johannessen. Today she has four guest rooms loaded with character—each has a private bath and water view. A large den downstairs, also boasting a stunning water view, is outfitted with books, games, a telescope, and comfortable chairs. Breakfast is included, and one morning featured the world's best Maine blueberry pancakes.

Popham was crawling with Hollywood types, on location in Popham filming *Message in a Bottle* the same week we were filming *Haunted Lighthouses*. We felt like small potatoes, but we got to see Robin Wright at our Bed and Breakfast, so nobody complained. A scene shot inside the Popham Beach Bed and Breakfast made it into the final cut of *Message*—see what you think of the place.

The Popham Beach Bed and Breakfast

207-389-2409

www.pophambeachbandb.com

Ghost of a Sea Captain
White River Light Station

Michigan

A salty ex-sea captain who tended his lighthouse for nearly half a century loved it so much he swore he'd never leave. Some people today believe the captain kept his promise.

I n the late nineteenth century, as the nation started rebuilding after the Civil War, shipping on the Great Lakes began its boom. America was demanding fresh-cut lumber and this heavily forested region obliged. Whitehall, Michigan, widely known as "The Lumber Queen of the World," was the supplier at the center of the action.

Practically overnight, Whitehall's once obscure little harbor became a major logging center and bustling port. Huge vessels carrying tons of fresh lumber steamed south, creating what may have been one of America's first traffic jams. Too many ships were coming and going, with no navigational aid. Prosperity had its drawbacks, and by 1871, conditions were downright dangerous.

Even with this alarming increase in ship traffic, few citizens of Whitehall came forward to speak for the installation of a lighthouse—in those days a device as critical as a traffic light at a modern highway intersection. Nobody spoke up except one man, a hardbitten former sea captain from England.

Following several tragic accidents on the water, town officials had once petitioned the federal government for lighthouse funds. But all requests were denied, and the issue died. It took feisty Captain William Robinson to come along and revive the cause and lead the battle practically single-handedly.

Born just outside London into a family of sailors and ship owners, young Robinson sailed the high seas with his father. Just as soon as he was old enough, he took command of his own ship. While still

Impact Television Photo

White River Lighthouse, Whitehall, Michigan, believed haunted
by the ghost of a former lighthouse keeper

in his twenties, his ambitions led him to America where he planned to make his fortune in the thriving lumber business. Instantly he was drawn to the Great Lakes region, where he finally settled in Whitehall, Michigan.

Upon arriving in Whitehall, Captain Robinson landed his first job in the shipping department of a major saw mill. He was a good worker and fast learner, and had no trouble getting a quick promotion to head of scheduling. Meanwhile, a pretty young woman named Sarah caught the captain's eye, and in less than a year they were married. Captain and Mrs. Robinson put down roots in Whitehall, where they would soon start raising a family.

But he couldn't get Whitehall's need for a lighthouse out of his mind, and he finally took matters into his own hands. Night after night, in the worst possible weather conditions, he stood on shore waving a lantern at approaching ships, transforming himself into a human lighthouse. Crews of passing ships named it "Cappy Robinson's Light." They laughed, but these skippers were eternally grateful.

In the mid 1870's, his ranting and raving finally captured the attention of the U.S. Lighthouse Service. Everyone in town jumped onboard the lighthouse band wagon, welcoming the announcement of a new light station for White River. Captain Robinson was a local hero. His stubbornness had finally prevailed; he was rewarded not only with a new lighthouse, but with the position of its first keeper.

"He was very proud of his position as first keeper," comments

*Karen O'Donnell, director, White River Lighthouse, who
hears strange footsteps and the thumping of a cane in the
dark hallways of the keeper's quarters.*

Karen O'Donnell, director of the White River Light Station, the
closest anyone can come to lighthouse keeper these days. Although
the beacon is deactivated, in a sense it is manned by Karen who is in
charge of the lighthouse and museum. "I sometimes think of myself
as a sort of keeper. Of course, I don't have to trudge up to the top of

213

the lighthouse every night to keep the light burning."

That's because there is no light at the top of the lighthouse. The old lens was removed years ago and placed on display in the museum beside other artifacts and a long wall of yellowed photos of the captain and his wife, two people Karen loves to discuss.

"When he arrived in Whitehall, the captain had no lightkeeper experience," she notes. "But he had always been out at sea. He knew everything there was to know about ships. The Lighthouse Service was so impressed with his strength and determination, they appointed him keeper anyway."

He and Sarah and their infant daughter moved into the tiny one-and-a-half story keeper's dwelling attached to the octagonal brick tower. The house was small even for the three of them. But Sarah wasn't about to stop having children just because the quarters were tight. Before long, the family grew to four, then five, then more. When they stopped counting, there were eleven children.

The captain adored them all. And they couldn't help but be close. Two adults and eleven children in two small rooms on the first floor and two rooms upstairs. But they did more than just get by. Under the captain's loving care, the family flourished and the beacon burned brightly.

Then without warning, life went dark. Still in her early fifties, Sarah Robinson suffered a brief illness and died. It was sudden and unexpected and Captain Robinson was devastated.

"Sarah was a very dedicated wife and mother, and she provided great support for her husband," says Karen softly, speaking reverently about the couple as though she had actually known and loved them.

"They shared a lot of duties," she adds. "She did a lot of the chores in the lighthouse and he often helped with the children. And they were very affectionate toward one another, frequently holding hands and embracing, even in public—an unusually romantic pair."

Cappy, as Karen calls him, never really got over his wife's death. The loss came at a time when the youngest of their children had just moved out on his own—a time when the Captain was looking forward to enjoying more time alone with his wife. Now he had nothing left but memories—and his undying passion for the lighthouse.

The work continued to be demanding. Cleaning and filling the lamps, trimming the wicks, shining the brass, and washing the lens. The captain lost himself in his duties. He swept the galleries and dusted the stairways. He painted the tower and polished the glass. Busy from dawn until dark, he didn't have much time to dwell on his wife's absence, or his own loneliness. He didn't think about anything but his lighthouse. Heart and soul, he threw himself into the job, and it caused him to withdraw further and further from the outside world. Time raced by.

By the end of 1918, William Robinson was the oldest lighthouse keeper in America. Still he was prepared to stay on. But one dark day, only weeks following his eighty-seventh birthday, he opened a letter and saw his world crumble before his eyes. Not since his wife's death had he received such devastating news.

"The government decided he was getting a bit too old to do the job," explains Karen. "So in 1919, he was told he would have to retire. And Cappy knew that mandatory retirement meant forced eviction."

Here was a man who had struggled bravely and all alone for the construction of this light station—a man who went out on the shore and waved a lantern to direct ship traffic before it was built. And after all these years, he was still a man whose determination was as strong as ever. A half century after he had triumphed in his battle to create the lighthouse, Captain Robinson vowed never to leave it.

"He saw the handwriting on the wall. So the first thing he did was finagle his oldest grandson, also named William, into the position of keeper. In this way the Captain could continue to live in the building. Then he actually argued with his grandson about who would be in charge. He said something like, 'as long as I have two legs and can walk, I will continue to tend the light by myself.'"

But the government discovered his secret arrangement with William and issued an order for the captain to leave the lighthouse. "He fell into a deep depression," says Karen. "He didn't eat, he didn't sleep. But what he did next was the most amazing thing you can imagine. He willed himself to die."

"In so many words, the federal officials said to him: 'Your time is up here.' He took them literally. That night he laid down to sleep and never woke up." Karen grimaces her annoyance at the authorities for kicking Cappy out of his own house.

Captain Robinson was buried in a grave across the channel from the lighthouse, in what is known as Mouth Cemetery, which apparently got is name from its location at the point where the White River flows into Lake Michigan. The captain's final wish was that his body be buried next to Sarah's.

On moonlit nights, you can stand beside the lighthouse and look across the harbor's inky water at the little hillside cemetery. In the murky light you can just make out the grassy slope where Captain Robinson and Sarah lie buried in their graves. But their spirits are still lingering on this side of the harbor, at the lighthouse they loved.

"He still walks the place. He is definitely still here." Karen says seriously, her steady blue eyes gazing at me.

For fifteen years Karen has been director of the White River Station. A former teacher and scientist, Karen has always shrugged off things not explainable by the laws of physics. But when she moved into these cozy lighthouse quarters, her shrugs turned into an acceptance of the unknown.

"I would say that this place is spirited—definitely. I would say that Captain Robinson and Sarah are still very much present in this building."

As a matter of fact, it was during her very first night in the lighthouse that she began to suspect she wasn't living alone.

"It was close to midnight," she begins. "I was in bed reading.

My eyes grew heavy and finally I nodded off to sleep for a short while. I woke up to a noise. It was the sound of regular, almost methodical footsteps, with the intermittent thud of a cane. It was so real I was afraid I might have locked someone in the museum. I thought, oh no, it's a tourist.

"I turned on the light and called out. *Hello. Is there anyone there?* I paused and listened. The footsteps had stopped. I called again. *Hello.* Still no response."

"By this time, of course, I was wide awake. I got out of bed and walked toward the door, passing the wall of photos. One of the pictures caught my attention. Staring back at me from a smudgy old black and white photo was the captain sitting on the front steps of the lighthouse. I had never thought about it before, but I noticed his cane. I knew immediately what I had been hearing. My ghost walked with a cane."

From that point on Karen grew accustomed to his presence. She says she hears him inspecting the lens room, doing the rounds at night, then stopping at the second floor where the children used to be. "It's almost like a parent looking at the sleeping children," she smiles.

"I would say that he is a diligent ghost. He has a steady pattern. As he walked in life, so he walks in death. That's how I'm experiencing him, doing the rounds. Basically, he's repeating the same pattern that he lived every day."

She's familiar with the idea that poltergeists and spirits can cause objects to move, seemingly on their own. But Karen is still baffled by the museum's glass display case that presumably cleans itself. What is this unseen force that performs mysterious housekeeping duties in the still of the night?

"One afternoon I noticed the glass on the museum's display case was dirty. I thought, I'll get to it in the morning. But by the next morning I didn't have a chance. The glass was spotless. And a rag had been left on top of the case. I was dumbfounded."

This has become a ritual. She sees that the case is dirty, locks up the room for the night, and upon inspection the next morning, the glass is perfectly clean. "And definitely not by me," quips Karen.

Karen believes it must be Sarah helping her out with the cleaning chores—something she would have done in her everyday life. Is there a message here? Can the phantom cleaner be sending a signal? Does the spirit feel a need to communicate, albeit in a roundabout fashion?

"It's my sense that if we could have a conversation, assuming something like that were possible, the captain would say to me: *You have the same dedication that I had. I like what you're doing here. I like the fact that you also have a passion for this building.*"

Karen says she struggles with the oddity of it all. "I've always been a bit of a skeptic about this sort of thing—about ghosts, I mean. Now look at me. People must think I'm crazy!"

The fact that Captain Robinson and his wife may still be present in the house seems perfectly normal to Karen. The couple has warmed their way right into Karen's heart, as well as her life.

Along with the spirits, even a little romance sometimes creeps into the lighthouse. There's a window about halfway up the tower. On the inside, the window is inset with a wide sill carved into a seat, just the right size for two people to share. Today, Karen keeps a vase with fresh cut flowers resting next to that window.

"I have a sense that the Captain and his wife used to sit here," Karen muses, enjoying the seat and a view outside across the water. She smiles shyly and her freckles seem to glow in the little blush that enters her cheeks. A couple of years ago, something special happened that gave Karen further evidence that she had spirits here.

"A professor from a local university visited the lighthouse," she explains. She describes him as a soft-spoken man in his early forties. He wore a tweed coat and smoked a pipe, and he was writing a book. Karen can't remember what the book was about, but it didn't concern ghosts.

"While touring the lighthouse, he was drawn to the window seat. His eyes kept drifting toward that spot, even when we were speaking of other things. He finally made the comment, 'I feel a strong presence there.' Then he asked me, 'Was there a couple living here who were very much in love? I feel a deep love that used to be expressed in that place.' He pointed at the window seat."

"I got a chill," says Karen. "I thought that his observation was very spooky, yet very touching, too. It was a belief I had had ever since I moved in here," says Karen. "But I never told anyone. Now, here was this stranger confirming it."

It was comforting for Karen to discover another person who had these feelings. On the other hand, Karen still feared she might be getting a little too close to the edge, or "really out there" as she puts it.

Karen thinks a lot about what she hears on the stairs—the footsteps trudging to the top of the lighthouse on cold, dark nights, the unmistakable sound of a man dragging his bad leg down the hallway, striking what sounds like a cane on the bare hardwood floor. She says it's sometimes disconcerting and other times causes her to question her own sanity. But something else happened to convince her she wasn't losing her mind.

"I had some friends who I asked to watch over the place while I was traveling. I was planning to be away for three weeks. But I didn't mention the captain to them. It's not something you say to people when you're asking them to stay in your lighthouse. 'Oh, by the way, there's a ghost living upstairs!'

"Everything went according to schedule. They showed up and I took off. Three weeks later when I returned home, the first thing they asked was: 'Do you have a ghost in this place?'

"I laughed and said, 'Oh no, you heard him, too?' They described the sound exactly the way I hear it—like somebody elderly walking with a cane. That's when I knew I wasn't nuts. Now other people had heard the captain."

Perhaps other people have seen the captain, too. Or at least his spirit.

One afternoon a neighbor came by. He was a thoughtful man walking his dog. Passing the lighthouse, he stopped to see what all the commotion was about. He inquired politely: "Is this really going to be on TV?" We get this question wherever we go, of course. The television cameras and gear never fail to pique people's curiosity.

Soon the dog walker and I began chatting away when he surprised me with another question. "Did you know this place really *is* haunted?" He explained: "I see a light out here sometimes at night." He pointed to the beach behind the lighthouse, on the other side of a steep dune. "The light is moving, like someone is swinging a dim lantern over his head around in a circle. Like someone is signaling with the light. The real strange thing about it, there *is* no person holding the light. But I've seen it quite a few times."

Did the man know the story of Cappy Robinson's light—the human lighthouse? Never had a chance to ask him. His dog kept pulling on the leash, anxious to keep moving along, and they did.

I asked Karen if she ever feels frightened living in this haunted lighthouse? "Nothing I've experienced with the Captain and Sarah is scary. None of their little antics in the night has ever really scared me. Don't ask me why."

"Seriously, I think there's a harmony here. They are content. They're doing what they did in life and not exhibiting any of the frightful cliches we often attach to ghosts. This is the real thing. And it's a lot less unnerving than most horror movies."

"I feel calmer knowing they're here. It's almost like having a watchdog—almost like having someone survey the place to make sure everything's tidy and ready for the night." One of Karen's quirks, as she calls it, is to straighten up the picture frames on display in the museum. She likes to have everything neat and orderly, "not unlike Captain Robinson himself," she points out.

"In the morning when I prepare the museum for opening, I will sometimes notice certain pictures off kilter. They're always the ones of the Captain and his wife. None of the other frames are off. The pictures that are moved are skewed at such extreme angles that a logical explanation isn't possible. And there's no wind inside the house. No earthquakes or anything. And no explanation."

No explanation but a stubborn ghost—watchful, playful, and with no apparent plans to let go of the lighthouse he loved.

T r a v e l   T i p s
White River Light Station

This stately thirty-eight-foot lighthouse is constructed of Michigan brick and limestone. It stands sentry at White Lake's entrance into Lake Michigan, on the western side, less than an hour north of Muskegon.

Established in 1875, and automated in 1945, the light was decommissioned in 1960. Today the lighthouse is a museum owned and operated by Fruitland Township, which opens it to the public June through August and weekends in September, charging a small admission fee. Guided tours are available by calling ahead, but the place is so small, special arrangements are probably not necessary except for large groups. It might not hurt to phone ahead, though, to make sure someone will be available to answer your questions.

Aside from its significant interest as a historic landmark, it's the size of the place that makes seeing it worthwhile. You'll discover firsthand one of the greatest hardships of lighthouse keeping a century ago: an obvious absence of creature comforts and a claustrophobic keeper's quarters. If you've read the story about Captain Robinson's ghost, you'll wonder how in the world the Robinsons raised eleven children in here.

While we were filming at White River, the downstairs was occupied by Karen O'Donnell, the museum director, along with her young son and a large dog. Karen showed me how her life had become a study in the efficient use of small space. For example, she kept kitchen pots and pans and an exercise bike under her bed. The dog appeared to double as a security system, and was so big he must have slept standing up. It was no problem for them. These people and their huge pet were happy to be here—like the Robinsons, come to think of it.

To find the White River Lighthouse, take US 31 to the White Lake Drive exit, turn right and head west. At South Shore Drive, turn left and follow museum signs to the end of Murray Road. It's a little confusing, but we found plenty of neighbors anxious to help.

When you climb the tower and enter the lens room at White River, the first thing you'll notice is that the lens is missing. This beacon will never glow again. Somewhere in the past they removed the fourth order Fresnel lens and hauled it down to the second floor of the house. Today the lens is on display in the lighthouse museum. Other exhibits include photographs, paintings and marine artifacts.

White River Light Station
6199 Murray Road
Whitehall, Michigan 49461
231-894-8265

—ᴡ—

If you pass Muskegon and venture this far north without a place to spend the night, your choice is limited. We discovered an above average Ramada Inn on Colby Road, just off the interstate. Request a room away from the highway and you won't be troubled by annoying truck rumble. My room had a whirlpool tub, a luxury I enjoyed but didn't mention to the crew, who suspect I call ahead for special perks. I don't. Continental breakfast is included, and a hearty Great Lakes country breakfast is available.

Ramada Inn of Whitehall

US 31 at Colby Road

Whitehall, Michigan 49461

800-2RAMADA

—ᴡ—

When we're traveling, a dilemma crops up for us that you probably won't experience, unless you also drag several trunk-size camera cases and a ton of electrical equipment with you on vacation. For easier unloading and storing of this television gear, we often choose a conventional motel. But a bed and breakfast in Whitehall came highly recommended by a local lighthouse buff, and we were tempted.

The White Swan Inn, built in 1884 as the home of a local sawmill owner, is a handsome Queen Anne-style structure close to town as well as the sandy beaches of Lake Michigan. I understand the innkeepers pay close attention to every detail, from personalized room décor, to hearty breakfasts, including a house specialty: White Lake blueberry muffins.

White Swan Inn

303 S. Mears Avenue

Whitehall, Michigan 49461

888-WHT-SWAN

www.whiteswaninn.com

—₥—

🍽 Try the River View Café & Bakery on North Mears in Whitehall. It's casual and friendly. Fresh local whitefish for lunch and dinner is a specialty. Cakes and pies all baked on the premises are worth the extra calories. A rooftop deck offers a good view of the White River in summer.

River View Café & Bakery

115 N. Mears

Whitehall, Michigan

231-893-5163

—₥—

You can't visit White Lake without seeing the giant weathervane on Business Route 31 in Montague. They claim it's the world's largest weathervane, and who's to argue? At forty-eight feet high, fourteen feet long, and weighing 4300 pounds, it has to be. The operating weathervane is connected to a working weather station, and stands on the north shore of White Lake.

World's Largest Weathervane

Business 31

Montague, Michigan

231-894-8265

—◠◡—

❧ The Chamber of Commerce of Whitehall and Montague is very helpful. Call or email and they'll send you a travel kit.

Chamber of Commerce: White Lake Area

124 Hanson Street

Whitehall, Michigan 49461

800-879-9702

info@whitelake.org

Ghost Light
Old Presque Isle Lighthouse

Michigan

Rational people swear they've encountered ghosts in lighthouses. But what if the ghost is the light itself, when an empty lighthouse can't be darkened? What's going on when night after night it shines on—no bulb, no power, no explanation?

From the time it was topped off in 1840, the stubby white light-house on remote Presque Isle peninsula was doomed. Not that it wasn't charming and picturesque. It was all that and more. Attached to the tower was an English-style, white-washed brick cottage that looked like the setting for a vintage Hollywood romance film.

It just didn't work well as a lighthouse. At a touch over thirty-feet tall, it wasn't much good as a navigational aid. Skippers out on Lake Huron complained they could barely see its light. Harboring very little affection for this stubby light station, they called it "the mistake on the lake."

Clearly, somebody had goofed on this one. And for the better part of the next decade, the lighthouse board held countless meet-ings to grapple with the issue. When the verdict came down—unsuitable for service—it became the official word. The small light-house was indeed a big mistake, and it had to go. But another twen-ty years passed before that happened. Finally an impressive beacon was constructed about a mile to the north. And it was everything that poor Old Presque Isle was not—tall and handsome. This new white, conical tower took over in 1871—all 113 gleaming feet of it.

Surprisingly, the powers that be didn't issue orders to tear down the old beacon. But they did make it absolutely clear that the light was forbidden to shine again. Old Presque Isle Lighthouse was extinguished forever. Or so it was thought.

The diminutive beacon languished for nearly a hundred years. So little was done to maintain the property, it seemed like a miracle

Impact Television Photo

Old Presque Isle Lighthouse

the tower didn't just topple over into the weeds.

Through it all, some say miraculously, the crusty old tower survived. Humble and oddly proud, it somehow braved the harsh elements and human neglect. The old lighthouse stood dark and silent, the shimmering blue lake on one side and a dark forest of tall cedars rising on the other.

Who would have dreamed that someday Old Presque Isle Lighthouse would be reborn? It took a couple of dreamers—George and Lorraine Parris. This retired couple from lower Michigan took one look at the old lighthouse and fell head over heels in love.

The Parrises appeared to be typical vacationers at a Great Lake resort—out for a good time for a couple of weeks before they rushed back to the city for another year at the old grind. But George and Lorraine were far from typical. These were gutsy people, big-hearted and determined. So determined, in fact, they managed to talk their way into an appointment as lighthouse caretakers. And before they were finished talking, they had gained permission to move into the cottage adjoining the lighthouse.

But as the old saying goes, be careful what you wish for. The Parrises had their work cut out for them. In real estate agent's jargon, they had a fixer upper on their hands—in need of a little TLC. In reality, from top to bottom, this place needed more than tender love could *ever* do for it.

The Parrises dove in with both feet and a ton of elbow grease. Lorraine cleaned and painted, George fixed leaks, patched the roof, and chased a flock of birds out of the attic.

One of George's biggest jobs was electrical. As official caretaker, George was placed under the direct supervision of the U.S. Coast Guard. And their first order to him was short and sweet: decommission the light immediately. In other words, make sure nobody can ever turn the light on in this beacon again—period. Although struck from navigational charts for all these years, the light actually worked, and the Coast Guard demanded George's assurance that it would not come on some night by accident, creating confusion for boaters on the lake, perhaps even causing a disaster.

George followed orders and went to work. He ripped out the spaghetti-like mess of wires and yanked the ancient bulb out by its roots. Now it was official. Nothing remained inside the tower but a hand-chiseled stone staircase and darkened lens at its top.

Meanwhile, the little lighthouse and cottage were becoming a cozy home for George and Lorraine. The couple's bond with their lighthouse grew stronger everyday—and their retirement turned into a dream. They now possessed everything they ever wanted, with hardly a care in the world and a private lighthouse by the lake to call home.

It was like winning the lottery, Lorraine later told me, a fairy tale turned into a reality, and they planned to live here happily ever after. For a dozen years, they did just that. But one hard winter the dream came to an abrupt end. George suddenly died.

Lorraine was grief-stricken. For several weeks after George's funeral, she spent nearly all her time shut up in the isolated lighthouse. Alone and depressed, she was overwhelmed by the responsibility of managing the property without George, but she didn't want to leave it either. She wasn't about to abandon the lighthouse she held sacred.

"We loved it here," she recalls, smiling, blinking tears away. "George and my love are still right here. And always will be here. I couldn't leave this place."

But then strange occurrences began to shake her conviction to stay. Four months after George's death, her loneliness and sorrow threatened to turn into something worse—a real nightmare.

"George passed away in January of '92." Lorraine says. "By the time May rolled around I was starting to adjust, getting used to being here by myself. One night, toward the middle of the month, I went to my daughter's house for supper. That's how I remember when it happened—when I got my first look at it."

When returning home to the lighthouse that night, Lorraine rounded a bend in the road and looked across Presque Isle Harbor. "I saw the light was on. I thought, *Boy, I'm going crazy. I really am.*"

Lorraine was stunned. At first she was nearly frantic. But she said nothing. Night after night the beacon glowed, a light she describes as a yellowish ball about the size of a full moon.

"It was on for about a month before I started telling anybody because I thought I was crazy. I thought nobody would believe me."

But they *did* believe her. And that's when she started to feel more comfortable with the light.

"It looks like there's a light up there in the tower," declares Ralph Gates, U.S. Coast Guard, retired. "Not a real bright light. But it looks like a light."

Lorraine's brother-in-law works on the ore freighter *Munson* that sails Lake Huron. He was once a skeptic—but that changed. "One day he rushed to the cottage and apologized to me. He said he saw it, too. Clear as anything, he saw the light from his ship."

"I called the Coast Guard," Lorraine says with certainty. "I said there is no power and no bulb in the lighthouse. They said, *No, Lorraine, you're crazy.* And I said, *No I'm not, it's on.*

The Coast Guard finally confirmed that the power was cut and the bulb removed. But they couldn't explain what people were seeing.

"There's a light that comes on, and I have seen it and I know it comes on," declares Jim Stebbins, who lives only a few doors away. His family once owned the lighthouse property.

"The Coast Guard came and investigated it and there's no reason for it. There's nothing." Stebbins is emphatic.

"I think there's a ghost out there," adds ex-Coast Guardsman Ralph Gates with a smile. "It's a *ghost!*"

Lorraine and the local authorities did everything they could to try to kill the light. "We've covered the lens inside. We put plastic all around it." Lorraine explains. "The light is still there."

What light? No one can figure it out. By any stretch of the imagination, there shouldn't be a light at the top of the tower. It's one of the deepest mysteries of the Great Lakes—but, by no means, the only one. This region has its share of supernatural phenomena. The ghost ship *W.H. Gilcher* has been sighted in the Straits of Mackinac, where it went down in 1892. People report that this old coal steamer regularly comes back to life on the foggy lake just north of Presque Isle near Mackinac Island.

Yet another ghost vessel appears on the water in this region— the phantom boat of French explorer Sebastion who apparently vowed to return to his fiancée—dead or alive.

And a mysterious sound has haunted the Great Lakes region for centuries. The eerie boom of a distant drum is often heard echoing across the lake. Called the "Ottawa Drum," many people believe the strange noise acknowledges each poor soul who has been lost in these treacherous waters.

The Dog Meadow Light is another Great Lakes mystery that keeps many people up at night trying to get to the bottom of the unexplained glow. Discovered decades ago in Wisconsin between Lakes Michigan and Superior, this bizarre glow lights up the waters of the Eagle River. It's been described by some witnesses as a "golden bull's eye." They say it moves on the horizon, sometimes changing color from white to red. No matter how hard they try, investigators have come up with no explanation for this strange phenomenon.

So ghost lights are nothing new in the Great Lakes region. And like many others, the mystery of Old Presque Isle may remain unexplained forever. Instead of trying to explain it, some locals have started to accept the strange light—even to rely on its glow. Lorraine tells us about boaters who actually claim it saved their lives.

"That light has guided boats into the harbor when it's so foggy you couldn't see," says Lorraine. "People have come in and told me if it wasn't for my light they wouldn't be here."

In one of the Great Lakes' dreaded pea-soup mornings, a small boat named *Temptation* found itself lost offshore. Blinded by thick fog, the craft drifted helplessly. Then one of its crew spotted a light and the captain followed it to safety.

It turned out to be the beacon at the top of Old Presque Isle Lighthouse—the light that wasn't supposed to be there.

Next day, the captain of *Temptation* wrote in Lorraine's log, "Your light saved our trip and probably saved our lives."

"It doesn't happen every night," says Harbormaster Mike Connelly, who speaks slowly and precisely, shaking his head like someone struggling with a mystery. "It doesn't happen to every boater. They keep asking us why and we don't have an explanation. I wish I had an answer but I don't."

Lorraine Parris thinks *she* does.

"He didn't want to leave here," says Lorraine. "He loved it here. George loved this light more than anything else or anywhere else. This was home."

Lester Nichols II, a neighbor who lives across the harbor from the old lighthouse, has a perfect view of the beacon, day and night. From his vantage point, he has no doubt that on certain nights he sees a light in the old tower.

"Yes, it's here," says Lester. "There is a light here. The word is that George is coming back and protecting the lighthouse he was at for so many years."

But according to Lester, this is one haunted lighthouse that really isn't scary.

"If George comes back as a ghost he is in fact a very friendly ghost. Anybody who visits our lighthouse need not be afraid of George. If George is here, he'll help them rather that hinder them."

Lorraine, too, is secure in the warm glow of Old Presque Isle Light. "I just think, well, he's here and he's guarding me. It makes me feel at peace."

As a rule, ghost stories don't come with happy endings. But the unexplained light in the beacon of Old Presque Isle makes this story an exception. And the warm glow in this empty lakeside lighthouse is enough to offer comfort for anyone's soul.

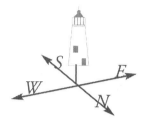

T r a v e l   T i p s
Old Presque Isle Lighthouse

You want to know what Presque Isle Peninsula looks like? Imagine a romantic movie filmed back in the 1940s—in black and white, of course. The chalky white lighthouse glistens in the summer sun. Under the tower, a little English-style dwelling is a double for the sea captain's cottage in *The Ghost and Mrs. Muir.* If Hollywood plans to remake that good old-fashioned drama, this is the spot. But if it's ever discovered by Hollywood, the place will never be the same.

Presque Isle—the name means *almost an island* in French—is a former lumber port in northeastern Michigan on the shore of Lake Huron. The town sits on the eastern shore of a small interior body of water called Grand Lake. Presque Isle Harbor, facing Lake Huron, is where the old lighthouse is located about a ten-minute drive to the north.

To reach Presque Isle from anywhere in southern Michigan, I-75 is your best route north. At the Gaylord Exit, pick up State Route 32 east to Alpena and Route 23 north from there. An alternative to

I-75 is the southern portion of Route 23 north, which hugs Lake Huron all the way up eastern Michigan. Unless you have time on your hands, don't repeat my mistake by crawling along Route 23 through small resort towns, past stoplights and strip malls. The interstate isn't pretty, but it sure moves faster.

At Alpena, SR 23 becomes a highway and in about half an hour you can be in Presque Isle, about twenty-five miles. As you pass the harbor marina, keep winding around the shoreline until you see a sign on your right for the lighthouse. It takes you through a forest of tall cedars to a point where the frosty blue water of Lake Huron comes into view. Soon the white-washed tower will peek at you through the dark green foliage. This beacon is the so-called ghost light—the lighthouse that just might stand protected by the spirit of a man who didn't want to leave it. If a little shiver crawls up your spine, you're not alone.

> Old Presque Isle Lighthouse
> 5295 Grand Lake Road
> Presque Isle, MI 49777
> 517-595-5095 (Presque Isle Chamber of Commerce)

—⋙—

In Rogers City, about twenty miles and a half-hour north of Presque Isle, the Buoy Restaurant on Third Street is recommended by locals who claim it serves the area's tastiest, most affordable seafood dinner. The specialty here is fresh, local whitefish, pulled right out of the lake and broiled with butter.

Buoy Restaurant
Third Street
Rogers City
517-734-4747

—∞—

If you're driving from Rogers City and points north, make a stop along the way at Presque Isle Township Cemetery. Here lie the graves of Bill Green, Charlie Priest, and Fred Prepkorn. It happened that these three pals, drinking buddies actually, made a pledge to one another. As each died the others would visit the grave, raise a bottle of whiskey in a toast, and pour a drink into their buddy's tomb. You'll notice that each concrete slab bears a tiny hole, drilled in the top to accommodate a cocktail. Come visit and try to figure out which buddy was last to go.

In Alpena we discovered a restaurant recommended for its home-cooked meals and no-nonsense service. If you flip for fresh baked pies, soup made from scratch, and delicious overstuffed sandwiches, head to *Someplace in Alpena* on West Chisholm Street. It's a quirky name for a down-to-earth restaurant, and you won't soon forget it.

Someplace in Alpena
West Chisholm Street

Alpena, Michigan
517-354-8325

—w—

Discover the story of Great Lakes maritime history told with interesting exhibits and media at the *Presque Isle County Historical Museum* on West Michigan Avenue in Rogers City. The imaginative displays on the *Edmund Fitzgerald* and other famous shipwrecks of the Great Lakes are worth the stop.

Presque Isle County Historical Museum
West Michigan Avenue
Rogers City
517-734-4121

—w—

The Presque Isle peninsula serves up a two-for-one special when it comes to lighthouses. About a mile down the road, the 109-foot Presque Isle Light looms over the open waters of Lake Huron with rightful authority. It's the new one—if you call 130 years old new.

It's a white, conical brick tower, first lit in 1871, and automated in 1970. The lens is a third order Fresnel and the beacon is still an active aid to navigation.

It's fun to climb, and if you've always wanted to get married in a lighthouse, they can arrange that for you, too. There's even a large meeting room for the reception.

New Presque Isle Lighthouse

4500 East Grand Lake Road

Presque Isle, MI 49777

517-595-9917

—∞—

❩ Both lights are open to the public from mid-May to early October. For more information contact the individual lighthouses or the Presque Isle Area Chamber of Commerce, 517–595–5095.

If you enjoyed reading this book, here are some other books from Pineapple Press on related topics. For a complete catalog, write to Pineapple Press, P.O. Box 3889, Sarasota, FL 34230 or call 1-800-PINEAPL (746-3275). Or visit our website at www.pineapplepress.com.

Lighthouses:

Guardians of the Lights by Elinor De Wire. Stories of the men and women of the U.S. Lighthouse Service. In a charming blend of history and human interest, this book paints a colorful portrait of the lives of a vanished breed. ISBN 1-56164-077-8 (hb); 1-56164-119-7 (pb)

Florida Lighthouse Trail edited by Thomas Taylor. A collection of the histories of Florida's light stations by different authors, each an authority on a particular lighthouse. Full of information on dates of construction and operation, foundation materials, lighting equipment, and more. ISBN 1-56164-203-7 (pb)

Guide to Florida Lighthouses Second Edition by Elinor De Wire. Its lighthouses are some of Florida's oldest and most historic structures, with diverse styles of architecture and daymark designs. ISBN 0-910923-74-4 (pb)

Bansemer's Book of Florida Lighthouses by Roger Bansemer. This beautiful book depicts Florida's 30 lighthouses in over 200 paintings and sketches. Engaging text, historical tidbits, and charming sketches accompany full-color paintings. ISBN 1-56164-172-3 (hb)

Key Biscayne: A History of Miami's Tropical Island and the Cape Florida Lighthouse by Joan Gill Blank. This is the engaging history of the southernmost barrier island in the United States and the Cape Florida Lighthouse, which has stood at Key Biscayne's southern tip for 170 years. ISBN 1-56164-096-4 (hb); 1-56164-103-0 (pb)

Lighthouses of the Florida Keys by Love Dean. Intriguing, well-researched accounts of the shipwrecks, construction mishaps, natural disasters, and Indian attacks that plagued the Florida Keys' lighthouses and their keepers. ISBN 1-56164-160-X (hb); 1-56164-165-0 (pb)

Bansemer's Book of Carolina and Georgia Lighthouses by Roger Bansemer. Written and illustrated in the same engaging style as

Bansemer's Florida book, this volume accurately portrays how each lighthouse along the coasts of the Carolinas and Georgia looks today. ISBN 1-56164-194-4 (hb)

Georgia's Lighthouses and Historic Coastal Sites by Kevin M. McCarthy. With full-color paintings by maritime artist William L. Trotter, this book retraces the history of 30 sites in the Peach State. ISBN 1-56164-143-X (pb)

Lighthouses of the Carolinas by Terrance Zepke. Eighteen lighthouses aid mariners traveling the coasts of North and South Carolina. Here is the story of each, from origin to current status, along with visiting information and photographs. ISBN 1-56164-148-0 (pb)

Lighthouses of Ireland by Kevin M. McCarthy with paintings by William L. Trotter. Eighty navigational aids under the authority of the Commissioners of Irish Lights dot the 2,000 miles of Irish coastline. Each is addressed here, and 30 of the most interesting ones are featured with detailed histories and full-color paintings. ISBN 1-56164-131-6 (hb)

Ghosts:

Haunt Hunter's Guide to Florida by Joyce Elson Moore. Visit 37 haunted sites, each with its "haunt history," interviews, directions and travel tips. ISBN 1-56164-150-2 (pb)

Haunting Sunshine by Jack Powell. Explore the darker side of the Sunshine State. Tour Florida's places and history through some of its best ghost stories. ISBN 1-56164-220-7 (pb)

Ghosts of St. Augustine by Dave Lapham. The unique and often turbulent history of America's oldest city is told in 24 spooky stories that cover 400 years' worth of ghosts. ISBN 1-56164-123-5 (pb)

Oldest Ghosts by Karen Harvey. Read about more St. Augustine ghosts. Includes interviews with people who share their homes with restless spirits. ISBN 1-56164-222-3 (pb)

Ghosts of the Georgia Coast by Don Farrant. Crumbling slave cabins, plantation homes, ancient forts—meet the ghosts that haunt Georgia's historic places. ISBN 1-56164-265-7 (pb)

Ghosts of the Carolina Coasts by Terrance Zepke. Taken from real-life occurrences and Carolina Lowcountry lore, these 32 spine-tingling ghost stories take place in prominent historic structures of the region. ISBN 1-56164-175-8 (pb)

The Best Ghost Tales of North Carolina by Terrance Zepke. The actors of North Carolina's past linger among the living in this thrilling collection of ghost tales. Experience the chilling encounters told by the winners of the North Carolina "Ghost Watch" contest. ISBN 1-56164-233-9 (pb)